Philosophy as the Doorway to Wisdom

Donald DeMarco

En Route Books and Media, LLC
Saint Louis, MO

ENROUTE
Make the time

En Route Books and Media, LLC
5705 Rhodes Avenue
St. Louis, MO 63109

Contact us at
contactus@enroutebooksandmedia.com

Cover Credit: Sebastian Mahfood

ISBN-13: 979-8-88870-523-0
Library of Congress Control Number:
Available online at https://catalog.loc.gov

Dedication

This book is dedicated to the memory of my brother, Richard, who, at 82, was taken by God to a better place, leaving behind his wife and their four children who will dearly miss his care, counsel, and quirky sense of humor.

Acknowledgements

The author expresses his indebtedness to Tom, Joe, Paul, Angie, Deidre, Peggy, Chris, and Sebastian for their encouragement and assistance.

Epigraph

"Wisdom is the clear, calm, accurate vision and comprehension of the whole course, the whole work of God; and though there is none who has it in its fullness but he who *searches all things, yea, the deep things* of the Creator, yet *by the Spirit* they are in a measure *revealed unto us.*" . . . . . . St. John Henry Newman

"In the past, and even to this day, there have been so many programs promising 'healing' for the world and proclaiming the arrival of 'true' justice in men's dealings with one another. But none of these can be regarded as complete unless it is linked with the justification before God—which is the main foundation of all justice" . . . Saint John Paul II, *Sign of Contradiction*

Table of Contents

Introduction

"Lord, what fools these mortals be!" This line, which appears in Shakespeare's play "A Midsummer Night's Dream," has broad application. While foolishness is common, wisdom is rare. Here lies the paradox of the human condition: what we most need—wisdom—is scarce. What we least need—foolishness—is plentiful.

How do we attain wisdom? The Danish poet, Piet Hein, has a curious answer: "The road to wisdom? – Well, it's plain and simple to express: Err and err and err again less and less and less." This may be a case of backing into wisdom. Our modest treatise, however, offers a more forward approach. Philosophy, rightly understood, opens the door to wisdom. In this progression, one not only attains wisdom, but also captures philosophy in the process.

Philosophy, as it is treated in this book, is congruent with common sense, a virtue that, unfortunately, is becoming an endangered species in this turbulent world. We are assisted in our journey by luminaries such as Solomon, Socrates, Plato, Aristotle, Augustine, Aquinas, St. Teresa of Avila, G. K. Chesterton, Jacques Maritain, Bishop Sheen, John Paul II, and other lights who will guide us.

The doorway to wisdom should not be an arduous journey as long as one is equipped with the virtues of humility, honesty, persistence, and the moral strength to resist the allurements of the secular world.

Waterloo, Ontario
April 20, 2025

I

Philosophy

Love as the Path to Personality

In his book *Slavery and Freedom* (1944), Nikolai Berdyaev (1874-1948) makes the comment that, "Love is the path to the realization of personality." Berdyaev is an important Christian existentialist. Since this Russian philosopher may not be well known in today's world, a brief introduction is warranted. He combined, to an exceptional degree, the virtues of humility and courage. He broke with Marxism and affirmed the values of Orthodox Christianity. He was twice imprisoned for his views, and in 1922 was expelled from his country. In exile, he went to Berlin where he founded a Russian academy of Philosophy and Religion. He later moved close to Paris where he lectured in a similar institution. The thought and passion of Berdyaev is grounded in the Christian philosophy of Dostoevsky. He was a friend of Jacques Maritain and one of the centuries leading proponents of Christian personalism. Berdyaev and Maritain were both staunch critics of Soviet communism as well as anti-Semitism.

Berdyaev's assertion that love is the path to the realization of personality is rich in implication. As a mere individual, man suffers from isolation. He tries desperately to find himself through conformism or adaptation, but he remains trapped in his own egocentrism. As long as he sees himself as an individual, he fails to realize his true identity as a person. Personality is not determined by heredity or social influence. It lies in his freedom which is the possibility of achieving victory over a world of determination.

The existence of personality presupposes the existence of values that are supra-personal. Hence, God plays an essential role. There can be no personality unless there are higher values to which a man can rise. The egocentric man is a slave because his attitude toward everything is servile, to something that is a non-I. Personality involves an I-Thou relationship, that is, a communion between two persons. The Thou to which the I tends is another I. No communion is possible with an object. The essence of his book is the notion that we become slaves when all our relationships are with objects, a process he calls, "objectivization." Person-to-person relationships, which form true community, are based on the mutual freedom to choose personality over slavery.

Love refuses to conform to the world or to limit itself to politics. There are two kinds of love; one that ascends to something higher, and the other that descends into the world of human beings. Personality is realized in both loves. Man often prefers to be a slave, according to this Russian thinker, because freedom is difficult, whereas slavery is easy.

If there is such a thing as "tough love," there is also such a thing as "tough philosophy." Berdyaev's clarity can be a source of embarrassment to certain individuals who have achieved some measure of worldly success but have avoided the more important challenge of becoming a person. There are many who denounce slavery but fail to see how their own materialism is also a form of slavery. Few people want to be reminded of this. In Berdyaev's words, "In the objectivized world they love only the finite, they cannot bear the infinite." It must also be said that his "tough philosophy" is very much needed in a world where so many people neglect the cultivation of what is most important in their lives—their personality. Love is the courage to resist materialistic allurements and become what one is destined to become, that is, a real person. Berdyaev's Christian personalism is about freedom, spirituality, liberation, authenticity, and courage. These are qualities that the world applauds without understanding what they really are and how demanding they can be. And so, they settle for an illusion or, to use one of Berdyaev's favorite words, a "fantasy."

"I remain in Christ's Church," Berdyaev declared, "that is founded on love and freedom." In so stating, he shows a strong affinity with the Catholic Church. For Berdyaev, as well as the Catholicism, love is the path that gives one the freedom to be a person. Conforming to the pressures of society is inimical to the development of the person.

Catholic historian, James Hitchcock's 1979 book addresses the same problem that plagues the Church today. The problem is deftly included in its title: *Catholicism and Modernity: Confrontation or Capitulation.*" Is the Church strong enough to resist the seductions of the world or is it giving in, capitulating under pressure? Hitchcock cites numerous examples of how many Catholics, including religious, are conforming to the world's secular agenda. For example, he refers to a former president of the National Coalition of Nuns who publicly attacked an Illinois congressman for sponsoring legislation to prohibit the financing of abortions through Federal taxes. She criticized him for "pontificating over women's bodies," asserting that "women must make their own decisions, according to their own educated consciences." In another example, Hitchcock refers to a Jesuit on the staff of the National Council of Churches who characterized the Catholic position of abortion as "uniformly unecumenical and therefore disastrous." Vatican II left little room for debate on abortion, which it condemned as "an abominable crime."

"He who is not with Me is against Me," Christ stated in Matthew 12:30. Love of truth keeps Christians on the path to personality while, at the same time, being faithful to Christ. To the person who trades religion for politics, Samuel Johnson has offered a soft-spoken but devastating rebuke: "Politics, did not, however, so much engage him as to withhold his thoughts from things of more importance." We must be faithful to God and develop our personalities before we can be of any service to the world.

In Defence of Intelligent Design

St. Thomas Aquinas' fifth proof for the existence of God proceeds from a recognition of design in natural bodies to the intelligent designer who made them. This intelligent designer, for Aquinas, is God. The natural bodies act toward an end without any intelligence of their own to guide them. Their intelligence must be provided by another. "Hence," writes Aquinas, "it is plain that not fortuitously, but designedly, do they achieve their end."

In so stating, Aquinas provides an argument for intelligent design and at the same time refutes, among other things, Darwinian evolution by chance. What Aquinas offers is an argument. And like all arguments it is abstract and on this basis easy to dismiss. It is common for people to reject an argument, no matter how valid it is, by simply saying, "That's your opinion." Another way of rejecting an argument out of hand is to say, "I know somebody who has a different opinion." A person may reject an argument merely because it finds its conclusion disagreeable. Egotism, as well as scepticism, is pervasive.

The Scottish philosopher David Hume (1711-1776) was highly skeptical about reason, believing that it is inherently contradictory. He strongly rejected intelligent design because he thought that if there were an intelligent designer he must have been extremely inefficient having created a world as flawed is this one is. "The world," he wrote, "is very faulty and imperfect, compared to a superior standard; and was only the first rude essay of some infant deity who afterwards abandoned it, ashamed of his lame performance: It is the work of some dependent, inferior deity, and is the object of derision to his superiors." Hume's skepticism and rejection of intelligent design, nonetheless, has had a powerful influence on the modern world.

Stephen Jay Gould of Harvard University has made an interesting point concerning the giant panda who lives on a diet of bamboo. In order to strip the leaves off bamboo shoots, the panda must grip them in its paw using a bony protuberance that emanates from his wrist. Gould argues that a true intelligent designer would have given the panda a real opposable thumb. Therefore, Gould concludes, the panda's thumb must have evolved by chance. Gould neglects the high degree of design that goes into the panda as a whole. This line of reasoning is akin to a sportswriter reporting that, "Last night Wilt Chamberlain missed four foul shots," neglecting the more important fact that last night he scored 100 points.

The argument from imperfection ignores everything that is not imperfect. Michael Behe, in his book *Darwin's Black Box*, summarizes this specious, but common argument: "1) A designer would have made the vertebrate eye without a blind spot. 2) The vertebrate eye has a blind spot. 3) Therefore Darwinian evolution produced the eye." What is conveniently ignored is how the eye, given its extraordinary complexity, came about in the first place. One could easily argue that no intelligent designer would create beings that are destined to perish. Design is evident. This fact implies a designer, just as murder implies a murderer. Everything else that is not part of a design has a different kind of explanation, if there is any explanation at all.

It is easy to dismiss an argument, no matter how compelling it is, when it is framed precisely as an argument. An argument is not something that is visible. It is conveyed in the abstract. As such, it may not elicit acceptance. It may be convincing, but not convincing to everyone. The truth may not be compelling when it is represented by mere words.

More convincing than an *argument* is an *encounter*. An encounter with truth is far less dismissible than truth represented by a string of words. An encounter is existential; an argument is abstract. Let us consider the following example of an encounter with truth.

Whittaker Chambers (1901-1961) was a high-ranking member of the Communist Party. When his wife became pregnant, a crisis arose. Abortion was a commonplace in the Communist Party. It was considered to be nothing more than, "a mere physical manipulation." Doctors rendered the service for a small fee. Chambers expected a routine abortion. His wife thought differently. She took her husband's hands and burst into tears. "Dear heart," she said in a pleading voice, "we couldn't do that awful thing to a little baby, dear heart." Her preference prevailed. They had the baby.

One day, while feeding his daughter who was sitting in a highchair, his eye came to rest on the delicate convolutions of her ear, "those intricate, perfect ears." And then the thought passed through his mind: "No, these ears were not created by any chance coming together of atoms in nature . . . They could have been created only by immense design." Reflecting on his epiphany, he concluded that, "Design presupposes God. I did not then know that, at that moment, the finger of God was first laid upon my forehead." He abandoned the Communist Party, became a Christian and worked as a writer along with William F. Buckley.

No argument had persuaded Whittaker Chambers concerning how intelligent design implies an intelligent designer. It was an *encounter* with truth that he found not only meaningful, but irresistible. If the term "open-minded" has any significance, it means being receptive to truth, whether it is delivered in a valid argument or through an encounter. The intelligent design that he recognized in his daughter's ears led to his conviction that God is the intelligent designer. His experience also gave credence to the validity of Aquinas' "fifth proof."

In Praise of Rain

This essay is a refutation of the assertion that a person is dim-witted if he allegedly does not have sense enough to come out of the rain. Bathing in the rain can be therapeutic. It is, however, not without sympathy for a little boy's prayer, "rain, rain, go away, Johnny wants to go out and play."

It is a concession to those innumerable fans of *Singin' in the Rain* who understand how rain choreographs life and can assist in overcoming adversity: "I'm laughin' at clouds so dark up above; the sun's in my heart and I'm ready for love; let the stormy clouds chase everyone from the place; come on with the rain, I've a smile on my face." Kelly's romp in the rain was foreshadowed by G. K. Chesterton when he extolled the person who "kicks his ecstatic heels to heaven, and listens to the roaring rain."

In a similar vein, Fred Astaire expresses his affection for Ginger Rogers by singing Irving Berlin's romantic tune, "Isn't it a lovely day to be caught in the rain." Rain does not dampen true love. In fact, it can add to its sparkle.

A scientist will tell you what he thinks rain is, namely, "a form of precipitation where water droplets have condensed from atmospheric vapor and fall under the force of gravity." But only a poet or a theologian knows what rain really is. It is a gift from heaven, a symbol of love, and a proof of God's Providence.

In the mind of the theologian, rain is not from the sky; it is from heaven. "Yet he has not left himself without testimony: He has shown kindness by giving you rain from heaven and crops in their seasons; he provides you with plenty of food and fills your hearts with joy" (Acts 14:17). In the words of the prophet Isaiah (45:8), "You heavens above, rain down my righteousness; let the clouds shower it down. Let the earth open wide, let salvation spring up, let righteousness flourish with it; I, the LORD, have created it."

And if rain is a blessing, a drought is a curse. God's love is the sole source of rain. "Do any of the worthless idols of the nations bring rain? Do the skies themselves send down showers? No. it is you, Lord, our God. Therefore our hope is in you, for you are the one who does all this" (Jeremiah 14:22).

In the mind of the poet, rain falls pitter-patter on roof tops, dances on sidewalks, and slides slowly down windowpanes. It makes possible the existence of rainbows. It is an elixir that refreshes and a tonic that cools. Only a poet could say that "Tears of joy are like the summer rain drops pierced by sunbeams." Nobel Prize winning poet Pablo Neruda says, "I grew up in this town [Parral, Chile], my poetry was born between the hill and the river, it took its voice from the rain, and like the timber, it steeped itself in the forests."

Rain has a musical quality. It can range from a pianissimo that is a drizzle to a downpour that is a fortissimo. Chopin's *Raindrop Prelude* illustrates how persistent raindrops can play on the heart strings. We also hear the rain in Benjamin Britten's *Still Falls the Rain* and Claude Debussy's *Jardins sous la pluie*. In painting, we may think of Van Gogh's *Bridge on the Rain* and J. M. W Turner's *Rain, Steam and Speed*. And we cannot forget that "the rain in Spain stays mainly in the plain."

At one time, there was a depression on the street in front of our house. It would collect rainwater producing a scent would attract ducks. One day, I witnessed a mother duck leading her ten ducklings around our miniature pond. It was a sight to behold, one that I would never forget and one that was owed to rainfall.

Rain brings unexpected pleasures. G. K. Chesterton comments on "one of the real beauties of rainy weather," when "the amount of original and direct light is commonly lessened [so that] while the original and direct light is commonly lessened, the number of things that reflect light is unquestionably increased. There is less sunshine; but there are more shiny things, such as beautifully shiny things as pools and puddles and mackintoshes. It is like moving in a world of mirrors."

Gustave Caillebotte's masterpiece is called *Paris Street; Rainy Day*. The painting brings to mind Cole Porter's 1953 song, *I Love Paris* and the engaging lyrics: "I love Paris in the springtime; I love Paris in the fall; I love Paris when it drizzles; I love Paris when it sizzles." There is something about the capital of France that takes on a special glow in the rain. "Rain is grace," said the novelist John Updike. It enhances the atmosphere, courtesy of the cosmos.

G. K. Chesterton, whom we have quoted, is both a poet and a theologian. Therefore, he has much wisdom to share with us concerning rain, especially on its bright side. "If I count it Christian mercy to give a cup of cold water to a sufferer, shall I complain of these multitudinous cups of cold water handed round to all living things; a cup of water for every shrub; a cup of water for every weed?"

I can accept rain interfering with my picnic, delaying the baseball game, or spoiling my party on the patio. There is too much to be said, however, in favor of rain. And therefore, I will continue to sing its praises.

Pass It On

When we pass on, it is good to know that we have something to pass on. We are all familiar with the aphorism, "You can't take it with you." It is an act of kindness to give something to posterity. It is more blessed to give than to receive. It is most blessed to give without any possibility of receiving.

"When you give alms," we read in Matthew 6:2-4, "do not let your right hand know what your left hand is doing, so that your alms may be in secret; and your Father who sees in secret will reward you."

This passage in Matthew may have inspired the Rev. Henry Burton to compose a verse he called, *Pass It On*: "Have you had a kindness shown? Pass it on; 'Twas not given for thee alone. Pass it on; Let it travel down the years, Let it wipe another's tears, 'Til in Heaven the deed appears—Pass it on." Kindness inaugurates a path that leads to eternity.

A UCLA drama student performed a scene from *Annie Get Your Gun*. Her dream was to go to New York and establish herself as a stage actress. An important factor stood in her way. She did not have enough money to get to the Big Apple. In fact, her sister, mother, and grandmother had been living on welfare. After the show, she was standing at the buffet when a man, unknown to her, approached her and praised her for her routine. When he asked her what plans she might have she informed him of her dilemma. The unknown gentleman must have been quite impressed with her performance and offered her a loan of $1,000 to get started. However, she must abide by three conditions. If she met with success, she would repay the man with no interest within five years. That she would not reveal his name. And, perhaps, most importantly, pass on this kindness to someone who is in need.

Our young drama student in the ensuing years met with great success and was more than able to pass on the kindness that allowed her to get started. She became a star of stage, screen, and television, known to the world as Carol Burnett.

Dale Schroeder, we might say, lived a life that was the antithesis of the glamourous life accorded to Carol Burnett. The limelight was not his cup of tea. Born in Iowa, he grew up in poverty. He did not get his own bedroom until well into his adult years. He was a carpenter who worked 67 years for the same company in Des Moines. A man of simple tastes and exceptional frugality, he owned but two pairs of blue jeans, one for the work and one for church on Sunday. He never married, nor did he have any children of his own.

Toward the end of his life, he went to his lawyer, a man by the name of Steve Nielsen. He presented him with a plan for how his money should be distributed. He wanted to help kids go to college, something he was never able to do because of his dire financial situation. When Steve asked how much money are we talking about, Dale said, "A little shy of 3 million dollars." "I about fell out of my chair," Steve said, expecting just a few thousand dollars.

As planned, when Schroeder passed away in 2005 at age 86, the money went to finance college educations for 33 poor Iowan students, including men and women. Many have trained as medical professionals and teachers. The last student to receive the final

$80,000 of Schroeder's bequest graduated as a therapist in 2019. The beneficiaries are affectionately known as "Dale's Kids."

Dale Schroeder had but one request. "All we ask is that you pay it forward." Pass it on. "You can't pay it back," remarked Nielsen, "but you can remember him and you can emulate him." A group has been formed to ensure that the "pass it on" kindness of Schroeder will continue down through years so that it becomes a tradition.

The Latin root for the word tradition is *trader,* which means to hand down or transmit. In the Biblical sense, it means to hand down teaching from one generation to another. It is an odd feature of today's culture, that many people are suspicious of tradition. They are mesmerized by the ideology of progress to the extent that they believe that any tradition is a hindrance to it. They want to be "unburdened" by past traditions. No one, however, would question the validity and importance of the tradition of kindness and generosity that was inaugurated by our civic-minded carpenter from Iowa. He has helped to restore the good name of tradition.

"When you get a blessing pass it on" is a saying that has universal appeal. When blessings are circulated, society is enriched. A blessing has the inner potential of being immortal. It can remain alive as long as it is passed on. Kindness is its life-blood. It remains alive when it is given away. It benefits both the giver and the receiver.

The kindness of Christ has blessed Christians for more than two thousand years. It is an attribute of His immortality. He did not bequeath to the world money or property, but a light that continues to shine and be shared without ever becoming extinguished.

The Mythology of Baseball

"Now is the winter of our discontent made glorious summer." In writing these words that opened *King Richard III*, was Shakespeare alluding to the arrival of baseball? If he was not, his words bear a striking resemblance to what Bill Veeck, a former baseball owner has said: "There are only two seasons—winter and Baseball."

What gives baseball such cosmic importance that it can be likened to a season? Baseball combines several advantages over other sports. It is played outdoors in warm weather and proceeds at a relaxed and leisurely pace. Like the seasons, it is in no hurry. It unites itself with the slow passage of time. There are plenty of intermissions, which allow spectators time to purchase and consume hot dogs and beer. Baseball is more than a sport. It is a way of enacting a microcosm of life. It is a mythology than has come down to earth.

When they were young boys, Dwight D. Eisenhower, Mario Cuomo, and Robert Barron dreamed of being major league baseball players. None of them achieved his dream. Eisenhower had to settle for becoming President of the United States, Cuomo for becoming governor of New York State, and Barron for becoming a Catholic Bishop in the city of Los Angeles. What captivates the minds and hearts of young and very capable young lads to aspire to play baseball as a career? It is something that is larger than life, something of mythic proportions. It is to become a hero of the magnitude of Hercules or Achilles. Joe DiMaggio and Ted Williams were not mere baseball players. They became immortal icons.

Baseball, unfortunately, is in trouble these days. Salaries are astronomically high, players have little loyalty to their team, fans have a hard time keeping track of where the players have gone, and the gap between the rich teams and the poor is ever-widening. Although baseball is a team sport, it is played by individuals who are looking out for themselves. The mythology of the sport is in danger of disappearing.

Nonetheless, the playing field remains a battlefield. There is victory and defeat. As one writer has remarked, "Baseball is a game designed to break your heart." Losing is more painful than winning. In baseball, one comes face-to-face with adversity. According to baseball guru Theo Epstein, "Baseball is a game based on adversity. It's a game that's going to test you repeatedly. It's going to find your weaknesses and vulnerabilities and force you to adjust. That adversity, in the big picture, is a really good thing because it shows you where your weaknesses are. It gives you the opportunity to improve."

Casey at the Bat is an 1888 mock-heroic poem authored by Ernest Thayer. The "Mighty Casey," a player of mythic qualities, has a chance to win the game for the "Mudville 9". Despite expectations, he commits the sin for which there is no forgiveness. He strikes out! His failure to come through in the clutch casts a dark cloud over the entire town. The closing four-line epitaph reads as follows: "Oh, somewhere in this favored land the sun is shining bright, the band is playing somewhere, and somewhere hearts are light, and somewhere men are laughing, and somewhere children shout; but there is no joy in Mudville—mighty Casey has struck out."

Ernest Thayer, however, did not strike out. He produced the nation's most popular piece of comic verse, one that takes its place aside Johnny Appleseed and Paul Bunyon. He understood the cosmic significance of baseball and how a strikeout could rob an entire town of its joy.

Grover Cleveland Alexander achieved immortality when he struck out Tony Lazzeri, a member of the New York Yankees "murders row," to save a world series victory for the St. Louis Cardinals. How important was that strikeout? Alexander's Hall of Fame plaque reads as follows: "Won 1926 world championship for cardinals by striking out Lazzeri with the bases full in final crisis at Yankee Stadium." These words comprised more than 50% of the words engraved on the plaque.

There are moments in baseball that are of epic proportions. Bobby Thomason's dramatic homerun with two outs in the bottom of the ninth inning to clinch the 1951 pennant for the New York Giants is described as, "The shot heard 'round the world." The homerun was heard on the radio by millions of listeners including U. S. servicemen stationed in Korea. The immortal phrase was coined by Ralph Waldo Emerson in his 1837 poem, "Concord Hymn," to announce the onset of the Revolutionary War.

Ray Kinsella's 1999 beloved novel *Field of Dreams* has been described in a book review as "both a rich, nostalgic look at one of our most cherished national pastimes and a remarkable story about fathers and sons, love and family, and the inimitable joy of finding your way home." Baseball inspires such tributes. Home is not only where the heart is, but it is the finish line for our life's pilgrimage. The batter begins in a stationary position at home plate. His objective is to round the bases and return to home plate. If he is successful, his team is credited with a run. He is a modern Ulysses who left his wife, Penelope, and ultimately, through great effort, returned to her. Baseball is a cycle that mirrors life. The "home run" allows passage around the bases without interference. It symbolizes our most cherished ideal, to return home victoriously amidst cheers of congratulations. Baseball is best understood when it intimates its mythology.

II

Wisdom

The Doorway to Wisdom

The Magi from the East are traditionally known as the "Three Wise Men." This is an identity that has been ascribed to them, but not what they called themselves. It is always presumptuous to claim to be wise. Socrates understood this and thereby honored the elusiveness of wisdom by declaring himself to be unwise.

Because wisdom is the possession of a great good, it is highly desirable. St. Thomas Aquinas states in his *Summa Contra Gentiles,* that, "Of all human pursuits the pursuit of wisdom is the most perfect, the most sublime, the most profitable, the most delightful." Wisdom is more valuable than most people realize.

Early philosophers who sought wisdom called themselves "wise men". Pythagoras, recognizing that wisdom, in the strictest sense, belongs to God alone, coined the term "philosophy" which means "love of wisdom." In making this important change, he displayed his own wisdom since he understood that wisdom in its purity is beyond the reach of any man. In addition, he introduced the friend or lover of wisdom as a replacement for one who claims to be wise. Thus, the doorway to wisdom is love.

It is common to be suspicious of philosophy because it appears to be an abstract exercise. It is easily ignored, however, that philosophy begins with an act of love. Love unites the lover with the beloved. It is realistic since its object is the reality of the other. Love is also in the service of the other. It is the best activity we have to honor something other than ourselves while at the same time being profoundly related to it. Love never exhausts itself. The flame of love is never extinguished. Nor does love abandon what is loved. It is undying in its fidelity.

The lover of philosophy does not tire in his search of wisdom, nor does he possess wisdom in its entirety. Love is the doorway, so to speak, and it opens to something that is always valuable and never fully attained.

The first problem that people face concerning wisdom is how to be its lover. There are too many things that are more immediate to us than wisdom. We do not need to search very much to find pleasure and material items that give us comfort. These things can block our search at the starting gate. Yet, all these distractions leave us with a sense of frustration. Wisdom must be more that any of the things that we can acquire. The *Book of Wisdom* asks, "Wealth and boasting, what have these conferred on us? All those things have passed like a shadow, passed like a fleeting rumor."

Wisdom and knowledge are distinct, although they are often used interchangeably. No amount of knowledge produces wisdom. They exist on different planes. All the knowledge in the world fails to produce a gram of wisdom. In his poem *Choruses from the 'Rock,'* T. S. Eliot asks, "Where is the wisdom we have lost in knowledge?" Mere knowledge, he says, brings us nearer to our ignorance, and our ignorance brings us nearer to death, but not nearer to God.

God, not man, must be the ultimate goal of man. Secular philosophers have tried to make worldly success of personal achievement the end of man. Death, however, puts an end to any kind of success a man can attain. Wisdom, therefore, must look beyond death. Nevertheless, philosophy is not a futile activity. It can be attained, though imperfectly, and because of great difficulty. According to Jacques Maritain, the wisdom of man is acquired by the labor of the intellect "and it for that very reason that his wisdom is gained with such difficulty and held so insecurely, and that those who seek it should be called philosophers rather than wise men."

Man, by nature, desires happiness. The entire philosophies of St. Augustine and St. Thomas Aquinas revolve around the notion that this happiness, this ultimate end of man, is to be with God. This is a wisdom that the world may dispute, but it is confirmed by philosophical reasoning.

A philosopher seeking wisdom understands the difficulties involved. He is human and subject to error. He lives in a world where people dedicate themselves to an earthly happiness. He converses among people whose ideas fall short of wisdom. There is no reason for him to boast about whatever shred of wisdom he possesses. He knows that he possesses it insecurely. He resists the temptation to feel superior to others whose lives are darkened by the absence of wisdom. He realizes his solemn obligation to share his wisdom with others and understands how difficult that is to accomplish.

It does not seem reasonable that a Providential God would create a human being in His own image and then abandon him so that he could not find a meaningful life by discovering his path to happiness. Therefore, God bestowed upon his creature the gift of philosophy. In the words of St. Augustine: "*Nulla est homini causa philosophandi, nisi ut beatus sit*" (man has no reason to philosophize, except with a view to happiness).

Wisdom and Truth

The deepest wisdom contains truths that transcend our understanding. And yet there are truths that are understandable but found to be unacceptable. The story of Socrates' defense, as presented in Plato's *Apologia*, is an example of a good man who is condemned to death because more people voted against the truth than were in favor of it. His defense was extensive, eloquent, and reasonable, but not sufficiently convincing. By a vote of 280 to 221, the Gadfly of Athens was sentenced to death. Socrates expressed surprise that the vote was so close.

"I do not believe that the law of God permits a better man to be harmed by a worse," Socrates stated in his defense. But he was more concerned about the harm his sentencing would have on his accusers. "I am really pleading," he said, "to save you from misusing the gift of God by condemning me." He appealed to a truth, a daughter of wisdom, which was less than persuasive: "Nothing can harm a good man either in life or in death, and his fortunes are not a matter of indifference to the gods."

"God remembers the just" is an utterance that belongs to the wisdom of God. The travesty of a trial came to an end. Socrates spoke his final words: "Now it is time that we were going, I to die and you to live, but which of us has the happier prospect is unknown to anyone but God."

The *Apologia* is a classic, for it encapsulates a timeless theme. Is the ultimate injustice paid to man rectified by a higher agency? Does God, in his wisdom and mercy, lovingly receive good men and women who have been unjustly put to death? We await the answer with a burning desire. The fate of Socrates demands a wisdom that escapes our grasp. We have faith that evil does not triumph over good, that God does not allow murder to be the last word. We trust in a wisdom that we cannot apprehend.

On June 9, 1987, Pope John Paul II flew by helicopter to the Majdanek death camp outside Lublin, the site of the most horrific "medical experiments" of the Holocaust. After praying in silence at the memorial to the camp's victims, he signed the visitor's book which bore a text taken from *The Book of Wisdom* (3:1): "The souls of the just are in the hands of God."

How moving and meaningful are these 11 words! At the same time, how satisfying and joyful. They are immediately superseded in the *Book of Wisdom* by the following lines: "No torment shall ever touch them. In the eyes of the unwise, they did appear to die, their going looked like a disaster, their leaving us, like annihilation; but they are in peace." God has tested the virtuous and "proven them worthy to be with him; he has tested them like gold in a furnace, and accepted them as a holocaust."

It is most interesting, perhaps even fortuitous, that *The Book of Wisdom* employs the word "holocaust" in this particular passage. But in the context, it means that the virtuous people who will find peace with God in the afterlife have been purified. Its meaning here is the direct opposite of how it is usually employed.

The issues Socrates raised in his defense are answered in *The Book of Wisdom*. Socrates states that the fortunes of man "are not a matter of indifference to the gods." This citation remarkably parallels "The souls of the just are in the hands of God," as found in *The*

Book of Wisdom. Socrates and Solomon bear witness to a truth that belongs to the wisdom of God and is shared by people of faith.

Pro-life advocates have expressed concern over what happens to the aborted unborn child. Perhaps Socrates and Solomon would have us believe that they are at peace with the Lord. This is a most gratifying thought. God does not forget any of His human creatures. There is a truth hidden in the bosom of wisdom that abortion is not the end of life. The abortionist does not have the final word.

Marion Montgomery is an award-winning poet, literary critic, and novelist. In his book *The Truth of Things,* he refers to the conviction of Socrates as "this first student evaluation brought to terminal resolution by hemlock." Ironically, the "Hemlock Society" that existed from 1980 to 2003 was a right-to-die and suicide advocacy organization. The moral message of Socrates was turned upside down.

For Montgomery, the death of Socrates by a democratic procedure is an occasion for him to call into question the reliability of education in today's world. He would like to have the following motto cast in bronze and placed as paperweights in the desks of all board of education chairmen, presidents, deans, principals, department heads, and teachers: "The good teacher emulates Socrates and Christ, neither of whom was popular with the majority of his hearers, or wrote articles or books, nor held degrees—honorary or earned—from recognized institutions of lower or higher learning."

Education is, in the best sense, an advancement toward wisdom. Among its best teachers in this regard—Plato, Socrates, Solomon, John Paul II, and Christ—are often those who are excluded. These ambassadors of wisdom may not have degrees, but they should serve as educational role models for any teacher who solemnly and enthusiastically believes in education.

The Meaning of Wisdom

Wisdom is a slippery word, like love. It means many things. Philosophers have pondered over it and come up with a variety of definitions. Many of these definitions, unfortunately, are incompatible with each other. We would like to know what wisdom is in the highest sense of the word. God is wise. In what ways can we imitate or participate in the wisdom that belongs to God?

The word for wisdom in Latin is *sapientia*. The root of *sapientia* is the verb, *sapere*, meaning to savor or to taste. What does *sapere* have to do with *sapientia*? These two words seem to belong to entirely different levels of meaning, one being physical, the other, metaphysical. When God proclaimed, "Let there be light," He was conjoining the spiritual with the terrestrial. Perhaps wisdom itself is, in some way, a combination of the two.

According to a venerable adage, *Sapientia est ordinare* (it belongs to the wise man to order). St. Thomas Aquinas states that "Because wisdom is reason's highest perfection . . . it is proper to it to know order." The order to which the Angelic Doctor is referring is the best or most fortuitous arrangement of the parts. It requires a value—wisdom—that is higher than mere knowledge. It is a wise person whose marriage is preceded by friendship, love, and dedication in that order. Disorder can be calamitous. The concept of disaster is based on a dis-order among the stars.

Wisdom is one of the Seven Gifts of the Holy Spirit. It is bestowed on people from above. Yet there is the physical component to wisdom. Perhaps wisdom is our ability to savor all the things that

God has made as we relate them to their Creator. The poet William Blake may have alluded to this in his *Auguries of Innocence* when he spoke of our capacity "To see a world in a grain of sand. And a heaven in a wild flower. Hold infinity in the palm of your hand. And eternity in an hour."

It is said that a wise man hears one word but understands two. There is the object and what the object intimates. To savor the divine in the mundane requires wisdom. According to Pierre Teilhard de Chardin, "The great mystery of Christianity is not the appearance, but the transparence, of God in the universe." A hymn of St. Gregory Nazianzen reads as follows: "All things proclaim you—things that can speak and those that cannot . . . All things breathe you a prayer, a silent hymn of your own composing." St. Augustine has stated that there are two ways of looking at the world. One is as if nothing is a miracle. The other is that everything is a miracle. Wisdom follows the latter.

Wisdom, then, can be said to be the ability to savor or taste the imprint of God in everything that He has created. It combines the terrestrial with the super-terrestrial, the mundane with the sublime, time with eternity, and finite with the infinite.

In Plato's *Apology*, Socrates is in search of wisdom. He does not find it in those who claim to be wise, nor does he find it in himself. It is said that Socrates was wise to confess his absence of wisdom. Yet, this notion of wisdom is devoid of positive meaning. Socrates' declaration that he does not have wisdom does not shed light on the positive nature of wisdom. Socrates was wise, but only in a very limited sense.

In a practical sense, we say that a man is wise if, through knowledge, experience, and good judgment, he can navigate through the complexities of life successfully. Nonetheless, this is a species of wisdom that does not necessarily include God. The highest form of wisdom must include God in some way. Joseph Plunkett has offered the world a poem in the mystical tradition in which the poet finds Christ in the things of nature. The title—"I See His Blood Upon The Rose"—announces the essence of the poem and serves as the poem's opening line. The next three lines accentuate the first: "And in the stars the glory of his eyes, His body gleams amid eternal snows. His tears fall from the skies."

No degree of human wisdom can come close to the Wisdom of God. An infinite gap exists between finite man and infinite God. Consequently, no matter how wise a person may be, he should carry himself with humility. The Roman statesman Marcus Tullius Cicero was being wise when he said that "The higher we are placed, the more humbly we should walk." Wisdom and pride are incompatible.

The wise person understands how far away he is from the fullness of wisdom. He is also mindful of how easy it is for him to regress. In addition, wisdom can be pushed aside by strong feelings. In Shakespeare's tragedy, Othello's final words are, "I am one who loved not wisely but too well." Intensity of feeling, unaccompanied by wisdom, proved to be, for Othello, his tragic flaw.

Wisdom in the practical order follows the rule of *Sapientia est ordinare*. In the mystical order, as we have noted, it can identify the bounty of creation with Christ. We suggest, with the required humility, that the highest form of wisdom for human beings is the ability to savor the traces of God's wisdom that he has implanted everywhere throughout his creation.

The Wisdom of God

Many people who believe in God have little trouble accepting that He is eternal, mysterious, omnipotent, and one. Concerning the wisdom of God, however, they have their doubts. How can God be wise if He allows all the suffering that goes on in this world, which is said to be a "valley of tears?" If one were God, one might say to himself, I would see to it that suffering would either be minimal or non-existent. I would ensure that everybody would be happy. But only God is God.

It may be questioned whether the absence of suffering would remove an important obstacle in the path of happiness. In addition, even God cannot make people happy. Humans must find happiness through their own efforts that accord with God's will.

St. Paul forcefully condemns the wisdom of the world. "Let no man deceive himself. If any one of you thinks himself wise in this world, let him become a fool that he may come to be wise. For the wisdom of this world is foolishness with God" (1 Corinthians 3-19-21). It is presumptuous for anyone to credit himself with wisdom. We are finite creatures who were created from nothing. St. Thomas Aquinas has stated that human wisdom is a vanity and is purely relative only when applied to his nothingness, but not when it applies to his glory. We may seek wisdom and benefit from our seeking, but it is brazen to think that we have obtained it on our own.

In emphasizing the point, Paul reflects the mind of God: "I will catch the wise in their craftiness . . . The Lord knows the thoughts of the wise, that they are empty." The divine indictment against the wisdom of the world could not be stronger. One need not look very deeply into the world of politics in order to find confirmation of this statement. Nonetheless, if the wisdom of the world is foolishness, this does not mean, logically speaking, that God is wise.

The problem with those who claim to be wise is that they see things from below. They do not view things from God's perspective. In this regard, the philosopher Benedict Spinoza (1632-1677) offers us some important light. He maintains that our sense experience can be misleading. What he calls an "adequate idea" follows from one or another of God's attributes, viewed in its eternal aspects, or as Spinoza puts it, "*sub specie aeternitatis,*" without any relation to time. Spinoza reminds us how limited and unreliable our ordinary knowledge is. Although his view of God is considered unorthodox, he stressed the importance of seeing things from the perspective of eternity.

Human beings locate their "wisdom" within a short time frame. They cannot see what will unfold in the future. It is like granting a baseball team a victory while it is leading in the fourth inning. There is much more baseball to be played. Cleverness is not wisdom even though it may be effective at certain times. It suffers from the narrow basis of egotism. The various gains that people make in various enterprises can be credited to knowledge and experience, but not to wisdom. Given the fact that what we call "wisdom" God calls foolishness puts us in no position to judge His wisdom which is exercised from above.

Divine wisdom is the knowledge God has of Himself and of all things. By contrast, we are a mystery to ourselves and know very little. The lower cannot judge the higher. Concerning suffering in the world, God permits it in view of a greater good that can arise from it. Only He knows this greater God before it comes into view. Christ's suffering is redemptive. Fr. Reginald Garrigou-Lagrange, O.P., expresses the matter clearly and succinctly: "Looked at in the light of this world our savior's passion appears to us enshrouded in gloom, but how radiant it must be when seen from on high, as the culminating point of history, that point to which everything in the Old Testament led up and from which everything in the New descends!"

God has revealed His infinite wisdom to us in the person of the incarnate Word, in His life, preaching death, resurrection, and ascension. It is our responsibility to utilise the gifts of the Holy Spirit, which include the gifts of wisdom and understanding, so that we may by participate in God's wisdom. We cannot generate our own wisdom, but we can share in the wisdom that belongs to God.

Solomon is the one human being best associated with wisdom. God spoke to him in a dream and said to him, "Ask what you would like me to give you. Solomon did not answer immediately but pondered the awesome responsibilities he faced in ruling a large number of people. Finally, he made his request: "Give your servant a heart to understand how to discern between good and evil." Then, God said to him, "Since you have asked for this and not asked for long life for yourself or riches or the lives of your enemies, but have asked for a discerning judgment for yourself, here and now I do what you ask. I give you a heart wise and shrewd as none before you has had and none will have after you."

God is the sole and primary cause of wisdom. We can be wise only in relationship to that fount of wisdom. Whatever wisdom we may attain must be accompanied by humility, the effective enemy of pride.

A Mother's Wisdom

The Amazing Story of Thomas Edison

Thomas Alva Edison (1847-1931) is considered America's most prolific inventor. Edison himself, however, did not apply that term to himself. In his own opinion, what he did was to improve and perfect inventions made by others. That may explain why he was excluded from a series of inventors depicted on United States postage stamps in 1940, which included Eli Whitney, Samuel Morse, Cyrus McCormick, Elias Howe, and Alexander Graham Bell. He did appear on a 1947 stamp but was not identified as an inventor. Edison, however, patented more than 1,200 products. And his influence on shaping the physical makeup of the modern world is incomparable.

He was indisputably a genius, though he downplayed his gifts when he famously remarked that "genius is one percent inspiration and ninety-nine per cent perspiration." He was, indeed, a hard worker, got little sleep and could work long hours without rest. His life, however, was a conundrum and the object of many biographers and many disputes. Who was this prodigy known later in his life as the Wizard of Menlo Park?

We go back to his youth when he did not seem to conform to grade school regulations. When he was seven years of age, he spent about 12 weeks in a noisy, chaotic one-room schoolhouse with 38 other students of various ages and capabilities. His teacher, no doubt overworked, could no longer tolerate young Tom's persistent questioning and presumably self-centered behaviour. He judged that Edison's forehead was unusually broad and that his head was larger than average. He made it clear that he thought the youngster's brains were "addled."

One day, as the story goes, his teacher gave him a paper that he was to deliver to his mother unread. "My teacher gave me this paper and told me to give it to my mother," he later wrote. His mother was tearful as she read the paper aloud: "Your son is a genius. This school is too small for him and doesn't have enough good teachers for training him. Please teach him yourself."

Edison was 24 when his mother, a former teacher, passed away. When rummaging through sundry family items in the household, he came across a folded piece of paper tucked away in the corner of a desk drawer. He opened it and read the following words: "Your son is addled [mentally ill]. We won't let him come to school anymore." It is said that Edison cried for hours upon reading the real words the teacher had written. He then wrote in his diary, "Thomas Alva Edison was an addled child that, by a hero mother, became the genius of the century."

As one would expect, the mother, after reading the highly disturbing note, spoke to the teacher. But she did not receive a satisfactory explanation. Consequently, she decided to be her son's sole tutor. The home-schooling, presumably, went well and Thomas learned reading, writing, and math. The chemistry lab that her inquisitive son built in the basement, however, created some anxiety.

The good mother feared that her young prodigy might one day blow up the house.

A U. S. Library of Congress biography of Edison attests that a school administrator did label him "addled," an event that led his furious mother to remove him from school and teach him at home. Reflecting on his mother's dedication, Edison penned these words: "My mother was the making of me. She was so true, so sure of me, and I felt I had someone to live for, someone I must not disappoint."

Edison's mother, Nancy Elliott Edison, like any wise mother, did not want to discourage her son. No doubt, she had a sense of his special gifts and felt responsible for nurturing them. In an interview published in 1907 in a newspaper called T. P.'s Weekly, Edison gave lavish praise to his mother, reflecting on how willingly she became his principal teacher when he was very young: ". . . she was the most enthusiastic champion a boy ever had, and I determined right then that I would be worthy of her that her confidence in me was not misplaced."

It has been said that there are no better teachers in this world than parents are for their own children. No one will have the love, care, and attentiveness that parents have for their own flesh and blood. And what was the consequence of Nancy Elliott's home-schooling: As one journalist titled his article: "Thomas Edison's Mother's Letter Changed the World."

Let us say, simply, that a mother's wisdom is incomparable, irreplaceable, and unimpeachable.

Thomas Alva Edison passed away on October 18, 1931. Shortly before his demise, he wakened to the music of his favorite composer,

Beethoven (played loudly since Edison was also hard of hearing). Looking upward to his wife, Mina, he managed to say, in a haltingly, stuttering manner,

"I'm finished . . . It's very beautiful over there . . . Eternal God."

Some researchers have questioned the authenticity of the "paper." Nonetheless, even if it were a fiction, it serves as an embellishment to the wisdom of motherhood without detracting from it. Everything else in the story is well documented.

III

Witness

Witness to Hope

I had just completed *The Integral Person in a Fractured World,* which centered on Pope John Paul II's "Theology of the Body." All that was left to do was to do was type in the dedication: "This book is dedicated with humility and gratitude to His Holiness John Paul II: witness to Hope, embodiment of Faith, ambassador of Love." While I was writing this dedication the doorbell rang. I was visited by a young man whose name is John Paul. It was an unexpected visit and the only one he ever made to my home. I could not pass off this unlikely occurrence as being a matter of chance, for I had experienced other remarkable occurrences involved the now canonized saint.

It was April 2, 2005. I had been invited to speak at a conference. During an intermission, I was chatting with a former student of mine who was, at that time, studying law. I was recounting several remarkable occurrences I had had involving the Pope. Our conversation was interrupted by the announcement that Pope John Paul II had passed away. We looked at each other somewhat startled, though also saddened. I said to him, "You see what I mean."

It is said that a saint makes the Gospel luminous. I believe that on several occasions, I felt John Paul's luminosity. John Paul was said to have "charisma." This word is derived from *charis,* the Greek word for grace. Romano Guardini refers to is as meaning, "the release of loveliness." Another word that the media used to describe John Paul's character was *amiability.*

In 1994, when *Time* magazine named Pope John Paul II "Man of the Year," a small group of its editors and correspondents flew to Rome to meet and honor him. After a private audience, Thomas Sancton, chief of correspondents, made the following comment: "I felt something very special in his presence. One does sense that this is no ordinary mortal. There is something about him that surpasses charisma and personality. You don't have to be a Roman Catholic, or even a believer in God, to feel something almost mystical in his presence."

John Paul was a man of remarkable versatility. He was a world class philosopher, a theologian, a poet, an actor, a playwright, a linguist, and a skier. He was more than the *Man of the Millennium* (to cite the title of Luigi Accottoli's book on the Pope). He is a man for all ages. George Weigel, author of the definitive biography of the Pope, *Witness to Hope*, has predicted that John Paul's "Theology of the Body" is "a kind of time bomb set to go off, with dramatic consequences sometime in the third millennium of the church." Though he passed away 20 years ago, John Paul remains a pope of the future.

We would be remiss if we did not mention his extraordinary sense of humor. He could joke in whatever language he happened to be speaking. On November 11, 1993, after addressing a group of workers in Rome, he slipped on a newly installed piece of carpeting in St. Peter's Basilica and fell several steps. Although he was in pain, he said to the crowd on his way out of the hall, "*Sono caduto ma non sono scaduto* (I have fallen, but I have not been promoted). The late Sir John Gielgud, considered Britain's pre-eminent Hamlet, remarked that John Paul has a perfect sense of timing. Others have likened his sense of timing with that of Jack Benny. At a synod in October 1994, his artificial hip joint was giving him problems. He tried to reassure the assembled bishops by citing the comment that Galileo allegedly muttered, "*Eppur' si muove*" (and yet it moves).

His writings have lasting value. Consider the following passage that unites the finite with the infinite in the context of truth: "The body, and it alone, is capable of making visible what is invisible: the spiritual and the divine. It was created to transfer into the visible reality of the world the mystery hidden since time immemorial with God, and thus be a sign of truth." How important it is for people to realize the implications of this statement. John Paul's "Theology of the Body" and his anthropological realism is more relevant today than when he was alive. His contribution to posterity remains in potency to be more fully understood. He is truly a pope of the future.

In 1976, during the Eucharistic Congress in Philadelphia, a certain man got up and gave a little speech which embarrassed everyone present. This man from a second-world country suggested that the hour is ripe for the final confrontation between God and the Devil, between the Word and the Anti-Word. Everyone coughed a little, and the man left. Two years later, he appeared on the balcony of St. Peter's in Rome introducing himself to the world as Pope John Paul II.

Being a witness to hope, St. John Paul will continue to serve the people of the world far into the future. He left the earth twenty years ago. Twenty years from now he may be better known than he is today. The many schools and institutions that bear his name will continue to study and promulgate his work. The abundance of books about him will ensure a lasting legacy. His pastoral visits to 124 countries planted seeds that will bear fruit in the next generation. The future will not see another like him. He was sent to earth by God, not for a mere 27 years, the length of his pontificate, but for time immemorial.

Bishop Sheen Now an American Hero

President Trump has proposed a National Garden of American Heroes, a sculpture garden honoring 250 "great figures of American history." Part of the motivation for such a garden is to respond in a positive way in a time when, in the President's words, "Angry mobs are trying to tear down statues of our founders, deface our most sacred memorials and unleash a wave of violent crime in our cities." He has pledged to build "a vast outdoor park that will feature the statues of the greatest Americans to ever lived." On the National Garden, he went on to say, "the devastation and discord of this moment will be overcome with abiding love of country and lasting patriotism."

The President's proposal calls for 250 statues of American heroes in 2026 honoring the 250th anniversary of the signing of the Declaration of Independence in 1776. Catholics are well represented. They include William F. Buckley, Clare Booth Luce, Antonin Scalia, Thomas Merton, Frank Capra, Vince Lombardi, Dorothy Day, Charles Carroll (the only Catholic signer of the Declaration of Independence), Venerable Fr. Augustus Tolton, Archbishop John Carroll, S. J., the first Archbishop in the United States, and the following American saints: Katherine Drexel, Junipero Serra, John von Neumann, Elizabeth Ann Seton, and Kateri Tekakwitha.

The selection of some of the honorees, however, has been met with criticism. Nonetheless, the selection of the Venerable Archbishop Fulton. J. Sheen should be applauded and free from any controversy. Sheen proudly combined his Catholicism with his patriotism, something that was questioned during his tenure and has been questioned throughout the history of America. The British philosopher, Bertrand Russell, for example, stated that a grave danger faced America, for the time will come when it will be Catholic!

In 1932, Rev. Fulton J. Sheen delivered a talk on patriotism on the Catholic Hour, sponsored by the National Council of Catholic Men with the co-operation of the National Broadcasting System and its Associated Stations. He began by pointing out the various reasons why many people felt that America and Catholicism were incompatible with each other. He cited the Church's opposition to divorce at a time when divorce was readily accepted by American society. He mentioned how Catholicism was regarded with suspicion since it accepted the Vicar of Christ who resided in Vatican City. He also drew attention to the fact that the Church was criticized since Her belief in another world might cause Her to neglect to the needs of the present one. In addition, he alluded to the fact that because the Church claimed to be a bearer of truth, it was allegedly incompatible with a democratic society.

The presumed incompatibilities that Sheen cited in 1932 are more vehement in America today given the broad acceptance of abortion, same-sex marriage, gender confusion, the pandemic of pornography, and euthanasia. Yet, the main point of his address, given nearly a hundred years ago, was that the Catholic Church has always been unwaveringly patriotic. America believes in equality, as written in the Declaration of Independence. But how does this equality come about? Surely, America has struggled mightily to achieve this ideal. "There is only one foundation for equality," Sheen declares, "and that is the Catholic doctrine that all men have been redeemed by the precious blood of Jesus Christ, that all men have been called to share His life, and that President and citizen, poor and rich, the mighty and the lowly, have been thought so much worth while that Christ would have died for the least of them." Equality extends to "the beggar in the Bowery and the man in the gilded apartment." Democratic equality, so difficult to achieve through political machinations, looks for a higher solution. It is the Catholic Church that stands for the love, peace, and brotherhood that any society so urgently desires.

Catholicism and America are not incompatible, as it is often believed. The Ku Klux Klan believed fanatically that America was only for Americans. Thus, they excluded blacks with an African heritage and Catholics with a connection to Rome. Their fanaticism led to murder in some cases. It is clear today, however, that patriotism can hardly be ascribed the members of the Klan while it is increasingly clear that Catholics can be patriotic. This is attested to by the fact that two candidates, popularly regarded as Catholics, were elected to the White House.

The selection of Venerable Archbishop Fulton J. Sheen as an American Hero is fully justified. Furthermore, his selection helps pave the way for other Catholics to understand that they do not need to compromise their faith in order to be American patriots. In fact, they can realize that being authentically Catholic allows them to be splendid American patriots, and even heroes.

In closing his 1933 address, Bishop Sheen made the comment that "Catholics will never love America because it is great, but America will be great because Catholics love her."

The patriotic expression, "God shed his grace on thee," from America's National Anthem, welcomes divine assistance. It affirms the compatibility of the secular and the spiritual. The Catholic Church teaches that marriage is sacred and that children are a blessing. The family is the basic unit of society. What damages the family damages the future. Catholicism is the great protector of the future. In strengthening the future by strengthening the family, as Sheen stated in 1932, "the Church is making it [America] stable enough to endure, that in the centuries to come it may draw down upon itself the blessings of a pleased and Almighty Father."

Making Aquinas Easier to Read

In the Prologue to the *Summa Theologica* of St. Thomas Aquinas, we find the following words: "Because the Master of Catholic Truth ought not only to reach the proficient, but also to instruct beginners (according to the Apostle: As Unto Little Ones in Christ, I Gave You Milk To Drink, Not Meat—1 Cor., iii. 1, 2), we propose in this book to treat of whatever belongs to the Christian Religion, in such a way as may tend to the instruction of beginners."

In the final sentence of the Prologue, the authors endeavor to "try, by God's help, to set forth whatever is included in this Sacred Science as briefly and clearly as the matter itself may allow." Nonetheless, despite this admirable, pedagogical aim, many students did not find Aquinas easy to read. This problem, we can say, is not so much due to the writing style of the Angelic Doctor as to the limitations of his inexperienced readers. This matter was taken seriously, even in the 13th century.

Thus, two years before Aquinas passed away, he was asked by his faithful friend, Reginald of Piperno, to write a simple summary of theology for those who find his massive *Summa Theologica* intimidating. Aquinas quickly set to work and produced *The Compendium of Theology*, dedicating it to his friend. Aquinas' plan for the compendium was inspired by St. Paul's teaching that "the whole perfection of the present life consists in faith, hope, and love. Therefore, his treatise would be divided into three parts. The first, dealing with faith, spans 246 chapters. He began the second section on hope, but reached no further than chapter 10. According to a close observer, "Friar Thomas d'Aquino wrote thus far, but alas prevented by death, he left it incomplete."

Thanks to the translation by Cyril Vollert, S. J., the *Compendium* is now available in English, published by Sophia Institute Press (1993). The editor renamed the book *Light of Faith*, which he deems "a title less ponderous that *The Compendium of Theology.*" Whether this work is easier to read than the *Summa* is not obvious and may best be left to the judgment of its readers.

The *Compendium* begins with an extensive treatment of God, beginning with his existence. The attempt to reach the uninitiated is evident on the first page. "But even the unlearned perceive how ridiculous it is to suppose" that things can be set in motion without a principal agent being involved. "This would be like fancying that, when a chest or a bed is being built, the saw or the hatchet performs its functions without the carpenter." This is a memorable line, and it can be used as fodder against Darwinians and various determinists.

Aquinas devotes three chapters to "diversity." He argues that God could not create a replica of Himself and thus created not one, but many things. "There had to be diversity in the things produced by God," he writes, "in order that the divine perfection might in some fashion be imitated in the variety found in things." His view of diversity might ruffle the feathers of modern egalitarians since he argues that order demands that some things be superior to others.

Freedom of choice is another issue that has caused a significant amount of confusion. Aquinas states that "the intellect desires and acts in virtue of a free judgment, which is the same as having freedom of choice." Human beings, because they have freedom of choice, are "not tied down to any one definite course." The intellect looks over a range of possible choice, like a diner looking over a menu before he decides what food he should select. He is under no compulsion to choose one item or another. However, since man is inclined toward what is good, he is under an obligation to choose what is good and avoid what is evil. Therefore, freedom of choice is not a terminal value. What transcends freedom of choice is the good that is freely chosen.

In his treatment of good and evil (chapter 108), he begins by stating, in a forthright manner, "Clearly, therefore, they are in error who seek happiness in various things outside of God." He then enumerates these things: carnal pleasures, power, honor or reputation, and the knowledge of created things. In the spirit of St. Augustine, Aquinas states that "man's desire comes to rest in the knowledge of God alone."

Concerning ultimate things (Heaven, Hell, and Purgatory), Aquinas makes the common sense remark that, "if there is a definite way of reaching a fixed end, they who travel along a road leading in the opposite direction or who turn aside from the right road, will never reach the goal." Life is a journey. The right road will take us to the right end. There is, it must be emphasized, a "right end" and a "wrong end." Aquinas offers a few easy-to-understand analogies. A sick man is not cured by being given the wrong medicine. A plant will not bear fruit if the procedure natural to it is not followed. A runner will not win a trophy or a soldier a citation unless each of them carried out his proper functions. There is a right way and a wrong way to live. If we chose the right way, we will reach the right end.

The *Compendium* is a helpful introduction to Catholic theology. It is, according to *The Thomist* (a scholarly journal), "A masterpiece of brevity, readability, and profundity."

Did Aquinas Really Prove that God Exists?

Let us begin by making it clear what Aquinas's famous "five proofs" did not prove. They did not prove that God is a loving God or even one who has the slightest concern for his creatures. The God whose existence he proved is the Supreme Being, but in the minimal sense, so to speak. It is what people in general mean when they utter the word "God."

Nonetheless, to prove that a being must exist who is not seen and is infinitely removed from any concept we might have seems not only daunting but presumptuous. It just seems unlikely that finite man can prove the existence of an infinite God. And yet, if we can overcome our inhibitions, we find that Aquinas's proofs are basically the consequences of common sense.

In addition, we must overcome a rejection of God on the flimsy basis that He does not correspond to our expectations of what a God should be. How can there be a God when there is so much suffering in the world, people say. Aquinas, as we would expect, is not naïve. He presents his five proofs in his *Summa Theologica*, Question 2, article 3. The first objection he records will seem familiar to many in the modern world. "If, therefore, God existed," people claimed in the thirteenth century, "there would be no evil discoverable; but there is evil in the world. Therefore, God does not exist." Aquinas answers this objection citing St. Augustine: "Since God is the highest good, He would not allow any evil to exist in His works, unless His omnipotence and goodness were such as to bring good even out of evil."

"This is part of the infinite goodness of God," Aquinas adds, "that He should allow evil to exist, and out of it produce good."

Christians should have no difficulty with the answers Augustine and Aquinas give since they believe that Christ's crucifixion is redemptive.

Aquinas's proofs all involve our mind moving from what we know to what we do not know. This movement demands nothing more than reason applied to evidence. For example, the sentence, "Our principal is a moron" appears on the blackboard. The principal, on discovering these words, is irate. But his anger does not cloud his reason. He knows that the blackboard cannot produce these words. Therefore, somebody must have written them. He wants to find the culprit and punish him. He knows he exists although he does not know his or her sex, age, or ethnicity. He has proof enough that someone wrote the inflammatory words on the basis of reason applied to evidence: The blackboard itself cannot produce these words. These words appear on the blackboard. Therefore, some agent other than the blackboard produced them. Reason is applied to this logical syllogism, and a certain conclusion is derived. This is a process we perform daily. Aquinas is simply applying reason to what he observes and draws a logical conclusion.

Let us limit ourselves to Aquinas's fifth and final proof which is stated briefly in a single paragraph. Aquinas, along with anyone else, observes that natural bodies which lack intelligence act for an end, either always or most of the time. Consider the Canadian goose. Somehow, it knows when to fly to a warmer climate. It also knows to fly south and when to land. In addition to all this, it knows to fly with other geese in a V-formation to reduce air resistance. Other geese in the flock of geese all know the same thing independent of any use of intelligence. Aquinas writes: "Hence it is plain that not fortuitously, but designedly, do they achieve their end."

Aquinas is ruling out chance since the complex, elaborate, and highly-integrated organization of so many natural bodies could not come about by chance. We should consider that chance presupposes order. Let us offer an example. I go to a supermarket and meet a friend. Our chance, or unplanned meeting, is the intersection of two lines of causality. Order must come first; chance occurs when two or more orderly sequences happen to come together. Charles Darwin relies heavily on chance occurrences to explain evolution, but he is unable to begin any explanation concerning how order was created.

Concluding his fifth proof, Aquinas writes: "Therefore some intelligent being exists by whom all natural things are directed to their end; and this being we call God." We might credit Aquinas with being bold for being willing to follow reason wherever it goes. The order and beauty of the universe is not self-explanatory. The explanation for its existence must lie elsewhere. It is because of the wondrous capacities of the human mind that we can affirm the existence of something as grandiose as God. It belongs to the philosopher and the theologian to have the courage to recognize the mind's extraordinary range.

We cannot confirm the existence of God in a laboratory. All this means, however, is that science has its limitations. Scientists know that the universe exists, but they do not know how it came to be. If citizens of the modern world had a little more respect for philosophy and theology, they would realize both their autonomy as well as their authority.

Aquinas manifests his confidence in reason while retaining a deep sense of humility. For the Angelic Doctor, our deepest knowledge of God is to know Him as "unknown."

Does a Saint Know He Is A Saint?

I had the pleasure of meeting Fr. Patrick Peyton, C.S.C., on two occasions. The first time was at a seminary in North Easton, Massachusetts, in the year 1961. I was given the great honor of being his altar server while he said Mass. At the last moment, however, the honor was given to a lad by the fortuitous name of Patrick Riley who, like Fr. Peyton, was born in Ireland. I accepted the switch as appropriate. It made Brother Patrick happy.

Thirty years passed before I met him again. This time it was at St. John Cantius Church in Chicago. During a question-and-answer period, someone in the audience dared to ask him if he thought of himself as a saint. Our image of a saint may be imperfect, but we are confident that humility must be part of that image. To everyone's surprise, Fr. Peyton said, "Yes, I think I am a saint." It was a shocking revelation, but after a second thought, I felt that if one is a saint, does he not have the right to declare himself a saint without violating the virtue of humility? Fr. Peyton, in a soft voice that had a tincture of sadness in it, said, "I have done everything that Mary asked me to do." He was not bragging; he was painfully answering the question as honestly as he could.

Consider his record. In 1961, he addressed a gathering of 550,000 people in San Francisco's Golden Gate Park. That same year he spoke to 600,000 people in Caracas, Venezuela. The following year, he prayed the rosary before 1,500,000 in Rio de Janeiro, Brazil. His message was always presented with utmost sincerity. For more than 50 years, he brought Our Lady's message to the four corners of the world. "The family that prays together stays together," along with "A world at prayer is a world at peace" identified him.

Saints are attractive, although, as history has shown, not to everyone. They have been martyrs. Fr. Peyton was an attraction in Hollywood and attracted high profile stars such as Bing Crosby, Loretta Young, Maureen O'Hara, Jack Haley, Irene Dunne, Grace Kelly, James Cagney, and Jimmy Durante. He became a television personality though his message to the world was simply to pray the rosary. In addition to "The Family Rosary Crusade," he established "The Family Theater for Television," which produced a full-length movie and a shorter one. He was also involved in the "Marian Hour" for radio and the "Family Rosary Newspaper."

Friends of mine agreed with me, that though we certainly lack the power or authority to canonize people, we nonetheless felt that Fr. Peyton had the charisma of a saint. He had the manner and the demeanor of what we believed to be a saint. He has made it to "venerable." Sainthood may come later. Venerable Patrick Peyton passed from the earth on June 3, 1992, at age 83, peacefully, while holding a rosary in a small room at the Little Sisters of the Poor Jeanne Jugan Residence in San Pedro, California. He is buried in the Holy Cross Community Cemetery at Stonehill College in North Easton, Massachusetts.

At the time of his death, he had preached to an estimated 28 million people, more than any other Catholic, and helped to produce over 600 television and radio shows. In June of 2001, the formal cause of canonization was introduced at the Holy See. On December 18, 2017, Pope Francis approved the Decree of the Heroic Virtue of

Father Patrick Peyton, C. S. C., thereby bestowing on him the title of Venerable.

IV

Philosophical Wisdom

Is My Existence a Necessity?

When I was very young and, of course, very naïve, I made a statement to my parents that was immediately and emphatically rejected. I said that if they did not sire me, another set of parents would. Therefore, I would have been reared in a totally different way. I knew nothing of genetics at the time, but my parents knew enough about that subject to realize that if they did not procreate me, no one else would have. Where would that leave me?

Their response was shocking. I had entertained the juvenile belief that it was necessary that I existed. If one set of parents did not produce me, another set would. My existence was necessary, not the identity of my parents. What this realization meant was that I was "contingent." I was not familiar with that word at the time, but I suddenly realized that my existence was attributed to a number of factors that also did not need to exist.

My parents had to meet, fall in love, marry, and at a certain moment in their life, the right spermatozoon had to fuse with the right ovum in order for me to be generated. Was I the product of chance, the coming together of a host of things that did not need to happen? I exist, but it was highly unlikely that this blessed event would ever have taken place. The odds were astronomically against me. Moreover, how could I be necessary if my parents were free?

It was a humbling thought for me to realize that I was a contingent being. It would have been so much more likely that I never existed. Yet I continue to believe that God knew what He was doing when He created me.

The 17th century philosopher, Gottfried Wilhelm Leibniz (1646-1716), considered "A Genius for the Ages," posed a fundamental question. "Why is there anything at all," he asked, "when it would have been much easier for there to have been nothing?" The fact that there is something, for Leibniz, is a sufficient and compelling reason for the existence of God. Being cannot arise from nothing. All of creation itself is contingent, dependent on the creative act of God.

God seized a moment in the life of my parents and brought me into existence. Perhaps I could think of myself as that particular being upon whom God wanted to confer existence. Therefore, I am not a creature of chance, but, as it states in the Bible, "an apple in God's eye." In one sense, I did not have to be; in another sense, God wanted me to be.

All this leads me to a sense of obligation on my part to offer humble thanks for my existence and to express my thanks by carrying out the duties that correlate with God's Will. I can also say that Love brought me into being. *Deo gratias* (Thanks be to God) is a response at the end of Mass to *Ite, Missa est* (the Mass has ended) for all the blessings received at Mass. It is also an opportunity to thank God for me, a contingent being, for creating me out of His divine freedom. If I were a necessary being, I would have no one to thank. It is, therefore, both an honor and a joy to thank God for rescuing me from nothingness and conferring upon me my very own existence.

St. Thomas Aquinas and other outstanding philosophers and theologians regard being as a composite of *essence* and *existence.* Each person is finite because he did not confer existence on himself. But he has an essence which is his humanity. Essence is limited to each being that possesses it. But existence is unlimited. Any number of beings can exist because God, whose essence is to exist, makes their existence possible. In this sense, my being is related to God and God is related to me through love.

Two mysteries, that are a basic part of Christian theology, confirm how love unifies beings. In the Most Holy Trinity, the Father, Son, and Holy Spirit are One, though they are three distinct persons. They are united through reciprocal love. In the Incarnation, Christ as human and divine are also united as one, though they, too, are distinct persons.

The work of love is primary and fundamental. It is a unifying force that the world fails to appreciate fully. The distinguished theologian Hans Urs von Balthasar draws our attention to the primacy of love in a most, eloquent manner. "The infant is brought to consciousness of himself," he writes, "only by love, by the smile of his mother. In that encounter the horizon of all unlimited being opens itself for him . . . " The infant is brought to the realization that there is someone or something beyond himself. It is an early awakening to the unlimited being that is God.

We are introduced to God through our mother's love. Therefore, it is profoundly sad to witness the exalted role of the mother being reduced to one who can make a choice for the child's extinction. Choice should not be separated from love. God chose each one of us out of love. God always says "yes" to what He creates. His will and intellect are not divided since He is One. He does not consider creating someone and then changes His mind and says, "No." For God, choice is always an affirmation.

I am a contingent being (as we all are), wholly dependent on God for my existence. My existence was not necessary, but from God's point of view I was wanted and freely brought into existence through love. That is enough for me. If I thought I was necessary, I would succumb to the vice of pride. But since I was sired through a free and loving act of God, I can eschew pride without feeling unimportant.

The Purpose of Time

"Time is money," said Benjamin Franklin, and "a penny saved is a penny earned." In his book of adages, frugality is a most important virtue. Time is an important resource that should not be wasted since it could be used to earn money and then to earn more money. Pennies are not from heaven; rather, they are from hard work. If the resourceful American founding father could look down from heaven, he might be pleased to see his image decorating the $100 bill. William James came close to Franklin's aphorism when he said the truth is the "cash value of an idea." "In god we trust," commented Jean Shepherd, "all others pay cash." Money talks and people listen.

We are solemnly warned not to waste this precious commodity. Yet people who find time on their hands find ways to "kill time" by engaging in frivolous activities that are readily available to them. Franklin, however, does have his disciples, and they are legion. "When I was young, I thought that money was the most important thing in life," said Oscar Wilde, "now that I am old I know that it is." Money is the very lifeblood of the economy. It divides the human race into the "haves" and the "have nots." J. Paul Getty summarized the purpose of his life by boasting that he became a billionaire.

The phrase "earning a living" is a justification for making money. It becomes a problem, however, when it interferes with having a life. Ebenezer Scrooge had this problem until he found happiness by giving money away. The desire for money can be intoxicating. It can be, in Shakespeare's words, "my more-having would be as a sauce to make me hunger more." How much money is enough? How do we come to understand that money is a means and not an end? It is a sobering thought to know that "you can't take it with you." Denzel Washington told the graduating class of the University of Pennsylvania that he had never seen a U-Haul following a hearse. Men can make counterfeit money, but it is wise to remember that the love of money can make counterfeit men. Affection for money does not lead to personal authenticity. Life is in the living, not merely in the earning. There must be a better reason for the gift of time than using it to pile up coin of the realm.

St. Josemaría Escrivá de Balanguer has placed time in the proper perspective. "A hardworking person," he writes, "makes good use of time, for time is not only money, it is glory, God's glory!" He speaks of two virtues that merge as one: resourcefulness and diligence. Resourcefulness is the use of the gifts that God has given us. They constitute our personal "resources." The word diligence is derived from the Latin, *deligo* which means to love, to appreciate, to choose something after careful consideration and attention. The person who is diligent does not rush into things. When he chooses the work that is appropriate for him, he uses his time wisely as his gift to God.

St. Escrivá alludes to the fact that Christ was a craftsman, an assistant to St. Joseph who was a carpenter. This human and divine activity of his indicates that our ordinary activities are significant in their own way. In fact, as the Spanish saint explains, "they are the very hinge on which our sanctity turns, and they offer us constant opportunities of meeting God, and of praising him and glorifying him through our intellectual or manual work."

Eddie Doherty was an American newspaper reporter, author of many books, and an Oscar-nominated screenwriter. He covered the 1927 Lindbergh flight to Paris. Later in life, at age 78, he was ordained a priest in the Melkite Greek Catholic Church. Fr. Doherty died on May 4, 1975 and is buried at Madonna House in Combermere, Ontario. The simple Cross that marks his gravesite reads, "All my words for the Word." It is a phrase that all Catholic journalists can take to heart.

The fact that our time and our work can be dedicated to God ennobles everything we do. Time is not money. It is the opportunity to glorify God. Our life exists along a timeline. It is calibrated in years. We will be judged by how well we used the time that was given to us. In this sense, time touches upon eternity.

The distinguished British journalist, Malcolm Muggeridge, in his later years became a Catholic. He regretted the many years allowed him as an author using his pen for frivolous purposes. Therefore, he titled his autobiography, *Chronicles of Wasted Time*. In his St. Augustine-like confession, he comments as follows: "It is painful for me now to reflect the ease with which I got into the way of using this non-language; these drooling non-sentences conveying non-thoughts, propounding non-fears and offering non-hopes. Words are as beautiful as love, and as easily betrayed. I am more penitent for my false words—for the most part, mercifully lost forever in the Media's great slag-heaps—than for false deeds."

God monitors our use of time. "Every idle word that men shall speak, they shall give account thereof in the Day of Judgment" (Matthew 12:36). At the same time, we should not discount God's mercy.

Time wasted cannot be retrieved. But as long as time permits, we can dedicate that part to the glory of God.

The Nobility of Common Sense

Karl Marx, in his *Treatise on Feuerbach,* composed a phrase that would change the world: "Philosophers invent theories of the world; we must change it." There is enough truth in the phrase to make it compelling, but it contains enough falsity to make it dangerous.

It is true that thinking must have some relation to action. Christ obliges us not only to hear the Word, but to put it into practice. Thought and action must go together. On the last day, we will be judged by what we did not do as well as what we did. Thinking about the problems of the day but doing nothing to ameliorate them is inexcusable.

Marx's ten-word challenge, however, is woefully misleading. It is a terrible injustice to philosophy to identify it as a way of "inventing theories." It is truly a caricature of philosophy to reduce it to a series of mere inventions. Philosophy, in its truest sense, concerns itself with the fundamental principles of reality. St. Thomas Aquinas expressed the matter simply and succinctly when he stated that, "The human intellect is measured by things so that man's thought is not true on its own account, but it is called true in virtue of its conformity with things" (*Summa Theologica,* I-II, 93, 1 ad3). Philosophers do not "invent," they observe and record. In this sense, they are recording secretaries of reality.

How the word "change" has echoed through the political world! Everyone wants change. No political movement has any wind in its sails if it does not urge change. This simple, everyday word, arouses people to action because they find their present situation to be unsatisfactory. Because all situations are unsatisfactory, change is regarded as a panacea.

The enthusiasm for change often eclipses the more important factor concerning the consequences of change. Will the results be better or worse for society? This is where philosophy enters the picture. We cannot change the world for the better unless it is guided by a sound philosophy. Just change the world has its contemporary phrases in "just do it" or "go ahead." However, we should look before we leap, a phrase that is closer to common sense.

If there is truth there is no need for change. But if there is error, there needs to be a change toward truth. Truth is not something esoteric, undiscoverable, or a mere opinion. It is the conformity of the mind with reality. And that is also a matter of common sense. Issues of common sense may not appeal to thinkers who want to dazzle the world with new ideas. Samuel Alexander, for example, held that space is God's body and time is God's soul. It was a new idea, but like all new ideas, they soon become old and then forgotten. But the truth remains.

It is a strange and startling fact, as G. K. Chesterton noted, that "since the modern world began in the 16th century, nobody's system of philosophy has really corresponded to everybody's sense of reality; to what, if left to themselves, common men would call common sense." The ordinary man may not be familiar with Husserl's phenomenology, or Berkeley's acosmic spiritualism, or Kant's transcendental idealism, but he is able to get around on the firm basis of common sense.

Bishop Fulton J. Sheen has remarked in his book *Philosophy of Religion* that a philosopher is unable to deal with the problems of modern society "unless he knows something about the organized thinking of common sense which is outside the moods of the times." Philosophy, therefore, is more than a mood, which can change from moment to moment. It is above the emotions and belongs to the tranquility of reasonable observation. In his critique on modern liberalism, *Slouching Towards Gomorrah,* legal expert Robert H. Bork comments that, "Being a mood rather than a philosophy, modern liberalism cannot be other than anti-intellectual." People are moody, the intellect is not. One can be "in the mood for love," but the intellect itself is serene and constant, like the compass that always points north.

Because common sense is common, it may not appeal to the philosopher whose taste is more aristocratic. Saint Thomas Aquinas is a philosopher of common sense and therefore a philosopher for the common man. Though common sense may be disdained, it is not without its virtues. It is realistic and practical. It is reliable and universal. It is fit for the common man as well as for kings and queens. Consequently, we can speak of common sense in terms of its *nobility.*

"There are three great essentials to achieve anything worthwhile," said Thomas Alva Edison. They are, "Hard work, Stick-to-itiveness, and Common sense." Edison, regarded as America's greatest inventor, did not exactly invent anything. Certainly, he did not invent anything out of the blue. He was always guided by common sense.

Ralph Waldo Emerson connects the common man and common sense with a higher rank than nobility. "Common sense," he wrote, "is genius dressed up in its working clothes." If, as James Madison remarked, "Philosophy is common sense with big words," that means that the best philosophers do not lose touch with common sense. The false word is a false word, but it is also a terminological inexactitude.

Changing the world for the better is a rather ambitious project. But if we begin with common sense and do not deviate from it, surely wonderful things will happen.

Recapturing Common Sense

Common sense is a universal gift. We all have it, though we do not always use it. Scientists have tried to quantify it but have failed. There is no need to quantify it. We know, instinctively when to employ it. We do not need assistance from science. Mother Nature has given us a reliable guide.

Common sense gets us through the day. We draw upon it to deal with unpredictable and even unique circumstances. It is also what allows the human race to survive generation after generation. We are lost without it, like a car that has run out of gas. It needs to be respected and not treated as a subject for tampering or, heaven help us, to be replaced. And yet, in today's world, common sense is in crisis.

We are most clearly aware of common sense when it is violated. John Smoltz, a National League pitcher, once tried ironing his shirt while he was wearing it. He did not save time in utilizing this method but was out of action for a few weeks. Violations of common sense are usually followed by immediate regret. "How could I be so stupid," one says to himself.

Common sense protects us, like the Ten Commandments, by a series of "don'ts." Do not smoke in bed; do not try to climb fences when you are past 80; do not eat potato chips during Mass; do not chew gum while you are eating cereal; do not swim in shark infested waters; and do not try to get the TV to work by kicking it. The list is endless. These violations of common sense, however, are seldom repeated. People learn their lesson and return, at least for the moment, to common sense, that safe harbor against its nemesis—common nonsense.

We are ruled not so much by the politicians in a democratic way, but by an oligarchy that believes that we can go beyond common sense. And so we have thrust into our society the notion that there are innumerable sexes, that all forms of sexual expression are equal, and that marriage is simply what people want. In addition, the liberal agenda calls for adopting political correctness and the trilogy of diversity, inclusivity, and equity to substitute for common sense. It also calls for defunding the police, decolonization, cancel culture, critical race theory, and the presumption that men and women are equal in athletic competition, all of which have proven to be counterproductive. Yet the beat goes on.

A school board in British Columbia sparked an outrage by removing Harper Lee's classic *To Kill a Mocking Bird* because it did not fit within the "equity lens" used to select books. Several authorities in education have advised removing the works of Shakespeare from libraries in the interest of greater diversity. The classics are judged as not being relevant to the times.

British Columbia journalist, Riley Donovan, has stated that, "Ideas like banning classic books and renaming schools do not arise from a ground-swell of public opinion—they are the result of a concerted effort of a small cadre of activists." While personal violations of common sense are quickly followed by regret, the ideologically-motivated violations of common sense continue for some time before people realize how foolish they are. There is some hope in this observation. People will have had "enough," and the tide will turn in the direction of common sense. Recapturing common sense, however, on a broad scale, will take time. Individuals, nonetheless, have their own role to play in the process.

Ideology stands in marked contrast with reality. An ideology is a set of assumptions that are unproven. Common sense is a fundamental, everyday kind of philosophy that is essentially realistic. A mother knows that she should nurse her child, just as a farmer knows when to plant seeds. We get by thanks to common sense. And this explains why we should fight for recapturing it so that it does not lead us in the wrong direction.

G. K. Chesterton wrote a book promoting common sense. It was based on the commonsense philosophy of St. Thomas Aquinas. American novelist Norman Mailer once remarked that if he ever met St. Thomas in the next world, he would commend him for that most excellent phrase, "the authority of the senses." Here is where Thomistic philosophy begins, by the five senses encountering reality. A Solipsist who believes that only he exists and no one else, has expressed surprise that this is not a more popular philosophy. Hegel believed that a thing can be and not be at the same time. Berkeley argued that to exist is to be perceived. St. Thomas, on the other hand, according to Chesterton, "immediately recognized the real quality in things; and afterwards resisted all the disintegrating doubts arising from the nature of those things." He knew that there were two and only two sexes, that marriage is between a man and a woman, that great literature should be read, and that the Gospel offers us a way of life. This is why Chesterton asserts that, "The fact that Thomism is the philosophy of common sense is itself a matter of common sense."

We need not go back to St. Thomas Aquinas to recapture common sense, though he most surely is its faithful ambassador. We have merely to look into ourselves and become more acutely aware of life in its immediacy. We are surrounded by deceivers. But we should not surrender to them the common sense by which we organize our life.

Losing Sight of the Obvious

The word "obvious" is the antithesis of the word "oblivious." While something that is *obvious* is easy to perceive, we are *oblivious* to that of which we are unaware. We are directly conscious of what is obvious. We are not at all conscious of that is oblivious to us. And oblivion is a state in which a person is not conscious of anything. One of the basic problems in education is that students have become oblivious to that which is obvious. William J. Bennett, author of the best-selling *The Book of Virtue*, and Secretary of Education under President Reagan, remarked that his basic task as an educator was simply to "restate the obvious." George Orwell has declared that "we have now sunk to a depth at which restatement of the obvious is the first duty of intelligent men." "Let me state the obvious," says John Kennedy, with evident frustration, "Illegal immigration is illegal, duh." Being oblivious to the obvious is a critical condition not only in education, but also in the area of morality. We must be able to see what is obvious before we can discover what is hidden. From the obvious we move to what is less obvious.

Walter Jackson Bate, in his biography of Samuel Johnson (1977) makes the comment that the key to the master moralist's power was his unblinking perception of reality, his refusal to put up with fashionable nonsense. Johnson had the ability, according to Bate, of attending to "that rarest of all things for confused and frightened human nature—the obvious." We may attribute this ability to a long line of thinkers from Aristotle to Aquinas to G. K Chesterton. Such thinkers are vitally needed when people become oblivious to the obvious.

I was enjoying the hospitality of my host a few years back when the next-door neighbor came in and happily announced that his synagogue now has female rabbis. "We are inclusive," he said, with an air of triumph. After he left, my host looked at me somewhat puzzled and asked, "What is wrong with that?" I replied, "We should never want to include either sin or Satan."

I could have provided a better answer. If this Jewish community is going to ordain female rabbis, it should have a better reason than simply because it is being inclusive; otherwise, they could ordain me as a rabbi. Inclusivity has no limit and imprudent inclusions could bring about utter chaos. Being "inclusive" is no reason to be proud. Being "selective" would make a lot more sense. But that is obvious whereas inclusivity is ridiculous. Our neighbor, however, was oblivious to the obvious fact that inclusivity is not a criterion for making important decisions. Slowly, American society is waking up to the idea that including more on no other basis than it is more is obviously nonsensical.

If, as it has been stated, 100% of bricklayers are men, should that figure be horrifying to those who champion inclusion, diversity, and equity? Should women be forced to be bricklayers in the interest of achieving equity? Should there be diversity among the bricklayers and include those who may not want to ply this trade? Or should the work go to the best qualified, even though that principle of selectivity is not consonant with inclusion, diversity, or equity? Common sense would favor what is obvious, not what may be viewed as politically correct.

The abortion issue provides an interesting example of not seeing what is obvious. All we know about the unborn through fetology and embryology points to the fact that the fetus that is sired by human parents and develops into what is incontestably known as a human being is a member of the human family and is a human being. Yet, many chose to be oblivious of that fact. John T. Noonan, Jr., states in his book *A Private Choice* that despite the evidence concerning the nature of the unborn, "we are reluctant to see it." Professor Noonan employs the pronoun "we" in the sense of "we Americans." The title of his book is ironic. There is too much connected with abortion—the unborn, parents, grandparents, possible siblings, medicine, law, and society in general—for it to be regarded as "private." A captain of a ship cannot make a private choice in scuttling the ship when there are passengers aboard.

Psychology teaches us about "cognitive dissonance" which shields us from things we do not want to know. But what is obvious remains obvious to those open-minded enough to witness the obvious. Neither the eye nor the ear may perceive what is present. Matthew 13:16-17 refers to this phenomenon in the following words: "But blessed are your eyes, for they see: and your ears, for they hear. For verily I say into you, that many prophets and righteous men have desired to see those things which ye see, and have not seen them; and to hear those things which ye hear, and have not heard them."

What we immediately see or hear brings us in touch with what is obvious. That is the beginning of a long journey. There is much to follow, as Matthew intimates. So much stands to be lost when the obvious is not perceived. We all want peace, justice, and equality. We might say, however, that unless we begin by agreeing on what is obvious, we will never attain these cherished values.

V

Philosophy in Absentia

The Most Terrible Deception

In his book *Works of Love*, the Danish existentialist, Sören Kierkegaard, makes a startling statement which is pointed enough to make the reader shudder. "To cheat oneself out of love," he writes, "is the most terrible deception; it is an eternal loss for which there is no reparation, either in time or in eternity." The reader stops in his tracks and asks himself, "Have I cheated myself out of love?" For Kierkegaard nothing is more important than love which alone conveys the meaning of life.

God has commanded us to love, to love our neighbor and even our enemies. Love is difficult. Have I avoided love, the reader asks, because it is difficult, perhaps even disagreeable? Have I cheated myself out of love and settled for something more pleasant, something more romantic and enjoyable? Have I mistaken love for admiration? Have I not had the time to love and attend to all of its consequences? Have I found innumerable ways to deceive myself? Kierkegaard is unsparing: "*So deeply is love grounded in the nature of man, so essentially does it belong to man*—and yet men very often find escape routes in order to avoid—this happiness; therefore they manufacture deceptions—in order to deceive themselves or make themselves unhappy." These escape routes, however, never satisfy and bring about unhappiness in various degrees.

Love is most certainly not lust, for lust is blind to the good of the other person. Human beings can be clever and mistake this vice for a virtue. Cleverness places too much concern on the self and in so doing loses sight of the other. Love can be fearful. C. S. Lewis has warned us in *The Four Loves*: "To love at all is to be vulnerable. Love anything, and your heart will certainly be wrung and possibly be broken." And so, Lewis goes on to say, we should wrap our heart "carefully round with hobbies and little luxuries; avoid all entanglements; lock it up safe in the casket or coffin of your selfishness." The net result, with which Kierkegaard would agree, "is damnation."

If C. S. Lewis seems too severe, Kierkegaard includes a redemptive factor. "If it is true that to love is the greatest happiness," he writes, "this is the greatest suffering—if it were not that being related to God is the greatest blessedness." It may be slightly unbelievable, yet it is true that happiness, love, suffering, and blessedness all intertwine. We should not want to cheat ourselves out of this formidable quartet.

The Gospel tells us that "the aim of our charge is love that issues from a pure heart and a good conscience and sincere faith" (I Timothy. 1:5). Where on earth does one find such love? During my days in graduate school, I was fortunate to have a landlady who was a special kind of human being. As a gentle soul with a warm personality, she was like a second mother to me. Her daughter explained to me how her father became seriously ill and was bedridden at home. The mother attended to her husband night and day, taking care of his every need. Then, one day, the inevitable occurred. The husband passed away. The daughter said to me, "Mom would have been perfectly happy to care for my dad in this way forever." Was this not an example of what the Gospel teaches? This fine lady personified the union of love, suffering, happiness, and blessedness.

Perhaps the most common way of cheating oneself out of love is to become attached to worldly goods which are, in Kierkegaard's words, "inconsequential things and therefore Scripture teaches that they, when one possesses them, shall be possessed as inconsequential things; but the highest neither *can* nor should be possessed as something inconsequential." Priorities are essential. Love comes first; everything else exists at a distance from love.

The most dangerous way of escaping from love, for the Danish philosopher, "is wanting to love only the unseen or that which one has not seen." In this instance, a person creates an imaginary ideal, which he finds, "intoxicating." "Mr. Right," however, does not exist, nor will he ever come into being. In loving one's neighbor, one loves imperfect man. There are no neighbors who are without some blemish. Love is remedial. It is a balm for the wounded. Kierkegaard warns against "seeking with fastidiousness."

Sören Kierkegaard is a philosopher, a theologian, a psychologist, and an astute critic of culture. In addition to his many gifts, he has a poetic sensibility. He brings his varied gifts together in the following paragraph in which he declares that God is the source of all love: "The hidden life of love is in the most inward depth, unfathomable, and still has an unfathomable relationship with the whole of existence. As the quiet lake is fed deep down by the flow of hidden springs, which no eye sees, so a human being's love is grounded, still more deeply, in God's love. If there were no spring at the bottom, if God were not love, then there would be neither a little lake nor a man's love."

Since God is the source of all love, we are deceived when we look elsewhere to find it. When we find God, we also find ourselves at the same time. Kierkegaard reminds us of both the power and the availability of love and warns us against cheating ourselves out of that which is most precious in our lives.

The Cure for Discontent

Sigmund Freud turned his attention to the universal problem of human discontent and wrote *Civilization and Its Discontents*. The celebrated psychoanalyst came to the conclusion that we are discontent because there is an irremediable antagonism between the demands of instinct and the restrictions of civilization. Therefore, according to the distinguished Austrian analyst, discontent is incurable. His conclusion, therefore, is most pessimistic.

Freud is a humanist and does want to provide help for people. But contentment, in his view, let alone happiness, seems unattainable. "Life as we find it," he writes, "is too hard for us; it brings us too many pains, disappointments and impossible tasks. In order to bear it we cannot dispense with palliative measures." So, what advice does he have for discontented human beings? He suggests three measures. The first is "powerful deflections," which cause us to lose sight of our "misery." The second is "substitutive satisfactions," which diminish it. And thirdly, "intoxicating substances" which make us insensitive to it.

People seek happiness, but misery is always in the way. How can this problem be ameliorated? Freud has the answer: "The service rendered by intoxicating media in the struggle for happiness and in keeping misery at a distance is so highly prized as a benefit that individuals and peoples alike have given them an established place in the economics of their libido."

When Doctor Freud employs such expressions as "the economics of their libido," one has the impression that he is not really talking about human beings but machines of some sort that have interacting parts. The 'drowner of cares,' for Freud, can help people to "withdraw from the pressures of reality" and retreat into themselves and find "better conditions of sensibility." Reality seems to be a bad place for human beings to inhabit.

Humans do not commerce with reality directly. They come in contact with it through civilization, hence the title of his book, *Civilization and Its Discontents*. For Freud, however, civilization is largely responsible for human misery. His view of civilization is sufficiently bleak that he suggests that "we should be much happier if we gave it up and returned to primitive conditions."

If civilization is bad for people, people themselves are bad for each other. Love does not seem to be the antidote for discontent since many people are, according to Freud, simply not worthy of love. His view of humans is as bleak as it is for civilization. "I have found little that is 'good' about human beings on the whole," he writes. "In my experience most of them are trash, no matter whether they publicly subscribe to this or that ethical doctrine or to none at all. That is something that you cannot say aloud, or perhaps even think." Nor does Freud spare the "virtuous man" who is really dreaming about the things that "the wicked man does in actual life." At the same time, he comments that "time spent with cats is never wasted."

Freud's analysis of discontent was one of the last of his books. It is pessimistic in the extreme and provides no realistic cure for discontent. Freud, as we know, was an atheist and, therefore, God is never part of his analysis. We find his perfect opposite on the subject of discontent in the person of Fulton J. Sheen. The good bishop, in a single sentence, provides the answer to the Freudian dilemma. "There is no surer formula for discontent," he writes, "than to try to satisfy our cravings for the Infinite ocean of Love from the teacup of satisfactions." To put things simply, man needs God and will be discontent without Him. Trifles will never satisfy him.

The finite can intimate the infinite, as in art, but it cannot contain it. The endless pursuit of material possessions or physical pleasures is more likely to bring about addiction rather than contentment. Christ tells us that, "Not by bread alone does man live" (Matthew 4:4). The word "bread" can be replaced by any other material item that produces momentary satisfaction. But a numberless series of momentary satisfactions does not add up to what the soul hungers for, which is God. The finite has no zenith. It always remains finite. It cannot emulate the Infinite. The German expression *schlechte unendlichkeit* means "bad infinity" because a countless accumulation of things that are finite becomes disappointing when it fails to reach that higher plane which alone can cure the problem of discontent. St. Augustine's dictum that our souls are restless until they rest in God places the human drama in its proper perspective.

There is a discontent which urges us to be creative, or to do something better. This has been called "divine discontent." But this form of discontent urges us to reach for something higher. The discontent of which Freud speaks is like an airplane that cannot get off the ground. Discontent in the religious sense serves as a motivation to be united with God.

Sigmund Freud and Saint Teresa of Avila agree on one point, namely, that this world is a source of discontent. They would disagree concerning the futility of discontent. The great Spanish saint has pointed out that "discontent with this world gives such a painful longing to quit it that, if the heart finds comfort, it is solely from the thought that God wishes it to remain here in banishment." Prayerful contact with God can ease our discontent in the world; union with God can cure it. Freud, despite his shortcomings, has given us, though indirectly, reasons to believe in God.

A Dozen Roses and a Dozen Thorns

We are experiencing a leadership crisis. In Canada, an ineffective Prime Minister has resigned under pressure. In the United States, one presidential candidate withdrew because of a cognitive disability, while another had virtually nothing to offer. The man who became president has frightened the wits out of many. And the Head of the Church in Rome, to put it lightly, has acted in a peculiarly non-Popish way. How do such unreliable individuals rise to the top of government? Why do the appointed leaders fail to lead?

For the ancient Greeks, three things were required to be a good leader: *logos* (the ability to reason well, *ethos* (moral character), and *pathos* (a sensitivity for others). It is not common for people to possess all three of these traits. But they seem entirely absent in the people who are running today's governments. In the current world, the three things that help secular candidates to be elected are money, charisma, and a good speaking voice.

Nor do we find capable leaders among the intelligentsia. This is why William F. Buckley once said that "I'd rather entrust the government of the United States to the first 400 people listed in the Boston telephone directory than the faculty of Harvard." Ronald Reagan was more pessimistic: "The most terrifying words in the English language are, I'm from the government and I'm here to help."

José Ortega y Gasset's book *The Revolt of the Masses* is a classic. It is an insightful analysis of an alarming trend in modern society, namely that the masses are seizing control of society. The "sovereignty of the unqualified" is his biting phrase. He pays special attention to what he calls "the barbarism of specialization." Prior to the arrival of the specialist, people could be divided, more or less, into the learned and the ignorant. The specialist, however, falls into neither category. The specialist knows more and more about less and less. The saga of a prominent physicist offers a harrowing example of this. He was a specialist in solid state physics. The more he knew about his subject the more he realized that matter is mostly porous. He entered this theoretical world and developed a fear that he would fall through the spaces. To avoid this tragedy, he wore snowshoes. Walking, for him, was like carrying his body across a tightrope. This may be an extreme example, but it does show how specialization can be a narrowing intellectual activity.

Ortega explains that the specialist is not learned for he remains ignorant of what is outside of his field of specialization. But he is not ignorant since he does know something about that small area that fits into his specialization. "We shall have to say," Ortega writes, "that he is a learned ignoramus, which is a very serious matter, as it implies that he is a person who is ignorant, not in the fashion of the ignorant man, but with all the petulance of one who is learned in his own special line." Such a person, in Ortega's estimation, is hardly prepared to lead or rule.

The specialist is a cousin of the expert. For Marshall McLuhan, the expert is the person who stays put while the rest of the world changes around him. One cannot remain an expert for very long.

The unreliability of the intelligentsia, the specialist, and the expert to involve themselves in governmental affairs leads to nostalgia for the common man. The jury system is based on the premise that in the court of law, a man should be judged by his peers. It is believed that there is a very good chance that justice would be rendered if a jury consisted of 12 such ordinary mortals.

The 1957 motion picture *Twelve Angry Men* is regarded as an exceptionally fine dramatization of what transpires among jury members as they wrestle with justice. It is well written and well-acted. But these are not its greatest virtues. Its chief merit is portraying realistically the kind of interplay between jury members whose interests in justice are compromised by their own prejudices and selfish concerns. It is a convincing argument against sentimentalizing the common man. The dozen jurors are "angry" because they find that the demands of justice are either too exacting or too inconvenient. In other words, the jurors are what we might expect if we took the first twelve names that appeared in the telephone directory. A passion for justice is not distributed equally among ordinary human beings.

G. K. Chesterton had his reservations concerning men who were specialists. He was once called upon to be a juror. The awesome responsibility of determining the guilt or innocence of a man, he mused, should not be left to the specialists. "When [civilization] wants a library catalogued," he wrote, "or the solar system discovered, or any trifle of that kind, it uses up its specialists. But when it wished anything done which is really serious, it collects twelve of the ordinary men standing round. The same thing was done, if I remember right, by the Founder of Christianity."

Chesterton is comparing 12 roses (the apostles) with 12 thorns (the angry men). But, with all respect to the great Christian apologist, was he looking at things through rose tinted glasses? The 12 apostles all became saints, not because they were ordinary men, but because they were nourished and sanctified by the Holy Spirit. The 12 were really 13.

Commencement Speakers Beware

2024 was a tumultuous year for commencement speakers. Some speeches were cancelled while others were relocated. There were walkouts, protests, and sharp repercussions. On May 11, Harrison Butker, an orthodox Catholic who plays for the Kansas City Chiefs, was roundly vilified for his thoroughly Catholic presentation at Benedictine College, a thoroughly Catholic College. He pointed out that "Some of you may go on to lead successful careers in the world. But I would venture to guess that the majority of you are most excited about your marriage and the children you will bring into this world." Denunciations were swift and severe. Some reactionaries wanted him fired and he was ostracized from a sports organization.

In that same month Jerry Seinfeld gave the commencement address at Duke University. But before he could utter a word, about 40 students walked out chanting "Free Palestine" amidst boos and cheers. Seinfeld's speech was essentially innocuous. "Pay attention. Fall in love. And most importantly you gotta laugh," he told the gathering.

At Harvard, more than 1,000 graduates walked out rather than listen to Maria Ressa, a Nobel Peace Prize Laureate. Both Israeli and Palestinian flags were raised. Even the president was booed. At the beginning of her 23-minute speech, she indicated how difficult it is to avoid being smeared. "Because I accepted your invitation to be here today, I was attacked online and called anti-Semitic by power and money because they want power and money, while the other side was already attacking me because I had been on stage with Hillary Clinton. Hard to win, right?"

Author Michal Smerconish was disinvited from giving a commencement address at Dickinson College after some students objected to a book he wrote 20 years ago in the shadow of 9/11. Had he given the address, he would have said to the graduates, "It's time for a national coming together. We have to surrender our superficial differences and re-establish social and economic connectedness." Controversial, right?

At Ohio State University, entrepreneur Chris Pan delivered a commencement speech that he later confessed he had written while on ayahuasca, a psychedelic drug that can cause hallucinations. At the University of California at Berkeley, dozens of students stood up from their seats inside Memorial Stadium with signs reading "Divest." At Virginia Commonwealth University in Richmond, dozens of students walked out during the graduation ceremony to protest the commencement address given by Republican Virginia Governor Glenn Youngkin. She had dared to criticize diversity, equity, inclusivity policies.

Humorist Garry Trudeau once said that "Commencement speeches were invented largely in the belief that outgoing college students should never be released into the world until they have been properly sedated." 2025 has emphatically proved otherwise.

There is a consensus of sorts agreeing that the very best commencement address was given by Steve Jobs at Stanford University in 2005. Jobs, the founder of Apple, never graduated from college, and his extraordinary life was a series of dramatic ups and downs. His advice to the graduates was this: "Sometimes life's going to hit you in the head with a brick. Don't lose faith. I'm convinced that the only thing that kept me going was that I loved what I did. You've got to find what you love." In his closing words, he said, "Stay hungry. Stay foolish."

In bygone years, there were a few gold nuggets contained in various commencement addresses. Alan Alda, in his commencement address at Connecticut College in 1980, said, "You have to leave the city of your comfort and go into the wilderness of your intuition." Denzel Washington at Dillard University (2015) and Stephen King at Vassar College (2001) were on the same page when they alluded to human mortality. The former said to the graduates that "You will never see a U-Haul behind a hearse," while the latter asked, "What will you do? Well, I'll tell you one thing you're not going to do, and that's take it with you." Arnold Schwarzenegger reminded the graduates of the University of Southern California (2009) to "Just remember, you can't climb the ladder of success with your hands in your pockets." George W. Bush provided some unassailable advice when he said to the graduates of Calvin College in 2005, "The future success of our nation depends on our ability to understand the difference between right and wrong and to have the character to make the right choice."

In contrast with the many protestors who were trying to accomplish things that are far beyond their control, Mitt Romney offered some down to earth, sensible advice to the 2024 graduates of Johns Hopkins University: "I would suggest that instead of defining yourself by career, that you choose to define yourself by things that are entirely in your control, your love for your family, your friendships, your faith, your service to others."

Commencement speakers for 2025 will face a daunting challenge. They can be tepid and avoid controversy or say something of substance no matter how controversial it may be perceived to be. A commencement speaker, if only for a few minutes, assumes the important role of a teacher, one who stands at the midpoint between the past and the future. And as a teacher, he must not only be wise during this time of tumult, but he must also be heroic. God bless the next platoon of commencement speakers who face a throng of people they do not know and advise them about a future they cannot predict.

The Commencement Address I Never Gave

I want to thank everyone involved who invited me to speak to the 2025 graduating class. I consider it an honor, but also a danger. The chances are that before I have finished my brief speech, you will have developed a fairly strong resentment toward me. That is the price I must pay for trying to be honest and deviating from the requirements of political correctness.

We all spend a great deal of our lives in a fantasy world. "Humankind can bear very little of reality," as T. S. Eliot has told us. Illusions are comforting. Reality is a problem. I would like to say something realistic today even though it carries the risk of alienating or offending you.

It is customary for a commencement speaker to forget the message he heard from the speaker who orated at his own graduation. The tradition of commencement speeches is not inspiring. They tend to be more of a sedative than an inspiration. The typical address lavishes undeserved praise on the graduates and expresses confidence that they, as no other graduating class in American history, will change the world for the better. A commencement address is a kind of love-in. No one gets upset. Or, at least, that is the plan.

The first thing I want to say to you is do not think that you are better than anyone else. Pride can lead you in the wrong direction. And, please, do not plan to change the world. The momentum created by a misguided world over thousands of years will not yield to your expectations. Select a task that is within your abilities, modest as it may seem to be.

The second thing I want to say is do not be angry. Historically, anger usually leads to violence. Anger is not the beginning of wisdom. I am not asking you to be insensitive to the world's egregious imperfections. I am simply asking you not to add to them. Anger has a way of making a bad thing worse.

You have graduated. Okay. Congratulations. That is not exactly a singular achievement. What you have learned at your school adds to the weight of your responsibilities. Let us not dwell too long on congratulations. And what are these responsibilities? They begin by living a life of virtue. A college education does not exempt a person from practicing certain virtues, especially chastity. Society has a warped idea of the nature of justice. Real justice honors the dignity of all human beings, including the unborn, the infirmed, and the elderly. Living a life of virtue with integrity is difficult. No one would dispute that. But it is the most personally rewarding thing you can do. Virtue is not an arbitrary set of rules. It is what gives you the strength and motivation to be truly yourself. The root of social justice is personal integrity.

Do not be easily offended, which is to say, do not cultivate a holier than thou attitude. Have the moral strength to abide nonsense without getting self-righteous. Be more concerned about not offending God. I dare say that if people made a conscious effort not to offend the Divinity, the world would surely be a better place.

Let us understand love and put it into practice. Love is the will and the effort to work for the good of others. There is no better way to improve ourselves than in loving others. At the same time, we should realize that love is the path to the realization of our personality. We are persons, not mere individuals. That means we are both uniquely gifted and socially responsible. Too much weight on the side of individuality can lead to selfishness, whereas too much attention to society can cause us to lose sight of our unique gifts. Life is a paradox. It keeps us humble, but at the same time, stimulates our growth.

Love your neighbor, which pretty much includes everyone. But there are more immediate demands placed on our love. Love all the members of your family, your friends, and even your enemies. This is the solid starting point. Life a life of love. No more can be asked of you. Your love will benefit the world, but in ways you may never know. Have faith in your love. It is contagious.

There will be for each and every one of you a second commencement. This is the greater commencement when you enter your afterlife. I realize that not all of you are Christians. The Last Judgment, however, puts things in perspective. How can my life be judged? This is an act that belongs only to God. We may hope that a divine being of some nature will one day say to us, "Well done, my faithful servant, now enter the joys of heaven."

I speak to you this day out of love. I have no intention to flatter you. But my love urges me to be honest and offer you, with a perhaps unrealistic hope, that my few words will stay with you, nourish you, and most certainly not offend you. You are children of God, emissaries of love, uniquely gifted mortals. I am not attempting to praise you, but merely to identify you. You are more than you may realize. Be true to yourselves. Go in peace into a troubled world, and do not be overcome by its seemingly uncorrectable problems. Thank you for your patience.

VI

Wisdom *in Absentia*

The Lure of the Secular World

Secular ideologies in the modern world are, generally speaking, Christian heresies. Like Christianity, they promise equality, liberation, and love. They believe in social justice, peace, and prosperity. Why should anyone seek these values in a formal religion when they can be obtained free of cost in the secular world?

A Christian heresy is not a substitute for Christianity, but its enemy. The number 6 is close enough arithmetically to 7 to claim to be equal to 7. From a theological perspective, however, proximity does not count. 7 represents virtue, as in the 3 theological plus 4 cardinal virtues. 7 is also the numbers of sacraments. The number 6 as well as in 666 belongs to the devil. There are 7 gifts of the Holy Spirit. God rested on the 7th day. The *Book of Revelation* speaks of 7 stars, 7 trumpets, 7 angels, and 7 churches. 6 falls short of seven and can never be 7. Analogically a heresy falls short of orthodoxy and can never claim to be higher than what it is.

Communism talks about equality and social justice. But it fails to include God and denies the dignity of the individual person. Secularism, despite its many merits, fails to acknowledge the importance of religion. Socialism replaces God with the State. The descendants of Descartes are trapped in their egocentricity while the sons of Nietzsche fail to honor their neighbor. The followers of Jean-Paul Sartre separate freedom from responsibility while disciples of Freud have no solution for discontent.

Each of these ideologies falls short of wholeness. They recognize the importance of some truth but do not prevent the lie from entering the picture. They are like a window that is 99% intact, but the single hole in it allows the cold to get in. We can bleed to death from a single wound.

Secular feminism is an interesting example of a popular ideology that simulates Christianity in several ways but can never coincide with it. It purports to be *apostolic, liberating, just,* and, most of importantly, free from the dreaded blight of *sexism.*

During my long tenure as a teacher, I have been in a good position to observe the grip that feminism has on various college students. They are proud and fearless. Their literature, conferences, and various kinds of meeting are committed to the promotion of feminism. Nonetheless, the apostolic ambitions of feminism run into an invincible roadblock. While some men identify themselves as feminists, many do so to placate women. But the feminist notion that men are essentially predatory and that the patriarchy is evil will not attract any sensible man to ally himself with the feminist movement. Some feminists (Valerie Solanis for one) have advocated the elimination of men. Christianity is open to everyone without exception.

Secular feminism is often labelled a "liberation movement." Many of its demands are in accord with justice, such as fair wages and being free from unjust discrimination. Yet there is little concern for a liberation in the area of morality. Feminists promote abortion with great zeal. Furthermore, they have difficulty denouncing pornography since it appears to be part of their newfound freedom. Their liberation is often a liberation from what they perceive as "the chains of morality." Christianity, on the other hand, advocates liberation from sin.

Secularism has appealed to many because it demands justice for all women. It contends, with logic and reason on its side, that women throughout the ages have been treated unjustly both at home and in the workplace. Betty Friedan asserts that the household for middle class women is akin to a "concentration camp." In her book *Just Love*, Margaret Farley argues that justice is central to sexual morality. But her notion of justice, although including respect for the identity and needs of others, is diametrically opposed to Catholic teaching which condemns contraception and homosexual expressions. She denounces John Paul II's "Theology of the Body" since she does not believe that the nature of the body (male or female) is a decisive element in determining the morality of sexual activity.

Sexism is cast as the great enemy to feminism. Discrimination on the basis of sexual identity is, to be sure, immoral. It is as immoral as discrimination against any other group of human beings. What feminists regard as this form of discrimination, unfortunately, is too broad to be taken seriously and often contradicts itself. There can be no doubt that feminists look at men with a jaundiced eye. Their denunciation of all men, as is the case in Susan Brownmiller's book *Against Our Wills* ("all men are rapists"), is itself decidedly discriminatory. Accusing the Catholic Church of being sexist for not ordaining women is a gross misunderstanding of the nature of Catholicism. Railing against barbershop quartets for being exclusively male is simply frivolous. In their zeal to overcome sexism, secular feminists use their muscle to destroy perfectly reasonable traditions and practices. While Christianity censures unjust discrimination, it does not use it as a broad sword to censure arrangements that are perfectly just and reasonable.

The lure of the secular world is based on several positive features that accord with Christianity. This lure, understandable as it is, omits certain values that are essential for a good life. Hilaire Belloc expresses the matter concisely and accurately in his book *The Great Heresies*: "Heresy is the dislocation of some complete and self-supporting scheme [include Christianity] by the introduction of a novel denial of some essential part therein." Today's heresies, secular feminism included, can be viewed as taking certain features that are in accord with Christianity and falling short of the truth, breadth, scope, and completeness which is her essence.

Abortion and the Golden Rule

The Golden Rule is one of the most honored of all moral teachings. It has the appealing virtue of even-handedness, or, to put it more philosophically, justice. "Do unto others as you would have them do unto you" has Biblical endorsement. Matthew 7:12 states, "In everything, do to others what you would have them do to you," and Luke 6:31 advises us to "Do to others as you would have them do to you."

The endorsement of the Golden Rule, however, goes far beyond sacred scripture. Buddhism states, "Whatever is disagreeable to yourself, do not do unto others," while Confucianism states, "Do not do to others what you do not want them to do you." The Golden Rule enjoys the reputation of being the most culturally universal ethical tenet in human history. It radiates equality, reciprocity, fairness, and mutual respect.

Abortion advocates have ignored the Golden Rule, having replaced it with the single word, "choice." But this "choice" includes the choice to reject the Golden Rule. It is not an open choice, but one that conceals one choice that is forbidden. This places the pro-choice movement at odds with the most universal moral precept the world has ever known. And yet, the movement has convinced many people of its moral legitimacy.

A young girl passed me by wearing a T-shirt proclaiming that she is a proud member of the "pro-choice generation." We do not expect T-shirt slogans to convey wisdom, but we might expect them not to be contradictory. Let us draw our attention to the peculiar use of the word "generation." Any generation exists only because the previous generation made it possible. To generate connotes producing something. What does abortion produce? We owe a debt of gratitude to the previous generation for making the present one possible. What would be the case for this young lady if her own mother had been a member of a "pro-choice generation?" Rather than hail the possibility of her non-existence, she should have been wearing a different kind of T-shirt, perhaps one that read, "Thanks, mom and dad, for making my existence possible."

Having an abortion is to do something to another that one would not want anyone to do to her. This seems to be a clear violation of the Golden Rule. Abraham Lincoln honored the Golden Rule when he made the remark that, "As I would not be a slave, so I would not be a master. This expresses my idea of democracy." Because Lincoln was opposed to being a slave, he was also opposed to enslaving others. He underscored the importance of this acceptance of the Golden Rule by stating that it is the basis of democracy where all are equal under the law and no man can own another.

The distinguished historian John Patrick Diggins, in his book *On Hallowed Ground*, condemns the misuse of freedom when it "presents the opportunity to enslave others." Likewise, concerning the abortion issue, it can be said that choice is misused when it chooses abortion and therefore exterminates another. Such an aberrant choice, at the same time, violates the Golden Rule as well as a fundamental tenet of democracy.

It is one of the peculiarities of the human mind not to see the obvious when seeing the obvious is of critical importance. The Golden Rule is just as incompatible with abortion as slavery is with democracy. This basic point needs to be restated again and again until the light dawns. Human beings can be slow learners. We need to re-learn how to honor that which is honorable.

The Protest against Life

The tragedy of the Sybil is recounted by Ovid in his *Metamorphoses.* Apollo offered to grant her a wish in exchange for her virginity. She took a handful of sand and asked for as many years of life as the number of grains of sand she held in her hand. Her tragic mistake was to wish for longevity but not eternal youth. The wish was granted and the Sybil, who lived a thousand years or so, continued to shrink with age to the point that she could be contained within a small flask. When asked what she wanted in her deplorable state, she answered, "I want death!"

T. S. Eliot chose this story as the epitaph for his most famous poem, *The Waste Land.* The Sybil, for Eliot, was a preamble to society's collective desire for death. "April is the cruellest month" because it is the renewal of life. Life is what the citizens of the waste land detest.

The March 6-12, 2025, issue of *The Epoch Times* includes a large photograph of a pro-abortion demonstration held in Amsterdam. Most of the protestors are women. A myriad of signs announce, "My Body My Choice," "My Life, My Voice, My Body, My Choice," and similar slogans. The photograph brings to life the article which contends that "'My Body, My Choice' Is Giving Girls the Wrong Idea About Life'."

In demanding abortion, were the demonstrators, like the Sybil, protesting not so much for choice as against life? They were making life subordinate to choice. In addition to that, were the women protesting against themselves, against who they are as female human beings?

In his best-selling book *Crossing the Threshold of Hope*, Pope John Paul II deeply lamented that, "In our civilization, woman has become, before all else, an object of pleasure." He recalled the climate of the time in Poland where he was brought up when there was great respect for women, especially mothers. Clamoring for abortion, however, is not a way of earning respect. It is a way of intensifying the notion that a woman is primarily an object of pleasure. A college student made this unfortunate transition clear when he said that he wanted abortion to continue because he hated using the condom. Abortion increases the likelihood that a woman would be seen as an object of pleasure. If abortion were illegal, or even culturally frowned upon, an important incentive would exist to discourage sex for mere pleasure. This incentive would also help to restore the notion that motherhood is something to be honored.

The women in the photograph were also protesting against being whole persons. In essence, they were reducing themselves, as John T. Noonan, Jr. has stated, to "becoming a solo entity unrelated to husband or boyfriend, father or mother, deciding for herself what to do with her child." The women were willing upon themselves a new identity conceived atomistically. They were aspiring to a loveless narcissism. They were choosing a fiction as their destiny.

A human being is radically incomplete without love. If a woman does not love her own child or the father of that child, whom can she love? We are not born to be narcissists, solo entities. Even on a crude materialistic level, we are highly dependent on others, for food, clothing, shelter, and innumerable other things. Our bodies are not solitary entities. We are communal, social, political beings. Love makes life livable. It is what converts a mere individual into a person, one who gives and receives love.

I look at the photograph with sadness. These women, so confident in their cause, are the descendants of the Sybil and citizens of *The Waste Land.* They are pleading for the death of their children and the truncation of their own identities. They will have more reason to complain about being treated as sex objects because that is exactly what they are inviting.

Did Christianity Invent Guilt?

It is not uncommon to hear someone berating the Church for loading him with guilt. This is a poor excuse for criticizing the Christianity since Christ came to forgive sins so that guilt will no longer plague us. Christianity did not invent sin. It recognizes it and is prepared to abolish it.

Sin, which is the prime cause of guilt, is a timeless and universal phenomenon. Therefore, people experienced guilt before Christianity was formed. Consider the following examples of how guilt was recognized and discussed in pagan Rome: "Guilt is present in the hesitation, even though the deed be not committed" (Cicero). "Alas! How difficult it is not to betray guilt by our countenance" (Ovid). "Men's minds are very ingenious in palliating guilt in themselves!" (Livy). "It is proper for the guilty to tremble" (Seneca). "By the verdict of his own breast no guilty man is ever acquitted" (Juvenal). These statements bear a sensitivity to the nature of guilt that accords very well with Christianity. In this regard, Christianity is indebted to these sensitive Roman thinkers.

Another misunderstanding concerning guilt is that it is false. There is such a thing as false guilt, and psychoanalysts are at pains to distinguish false from true guilt. Schopenhauer wrote about the sin of being born. Obviously, this is not an act that one commits. Some have been seduced into feeling guilty because they are Catholic or pro-life. People can be made to feel guilty even though they have done no wrong. True guilt is a person's recognition of his complicity in wrong doing. It can vary in intensity from regret that one has stolen a pen to Lady Macbeth for her role in the murder of the King. Her guilt was inerasable and devastating: "All the perfumes of Arabia will not sweeten this little hand." She died of unexpiated guilt.

A washing machine is loaded with dirty laundry. Its purpose is to get the various articles clean. No one criticizes the machine for harboring filth. When the last cycles are completed, the clothes are clean again. The action of the washing machine parallels the removal of sin. "If we claim to be without sin, we deceive ourselves and the truth is not in us. If we confess our sins, He is faithful and just and will forgive us our sins and purify us from all unrighteousness. If we claim we have not sinned, we make Him out to be a liar and his word is not in us" (1 John: 8-10).

Recognizing that we have sinned is far healthier than denying it or projecting it onto someone else. Comedian Flip Wilson's famous line, "The devil made me do it," unfailingly elicits laughter from his audience. Our faults are not in the stars, but in ourselves. The recognition that I am the agent of my wrongdoing should be followed by a sincere confession along with a firm promise of amendment. Christianity is a cure for sin, not its cause. The purpose of Christianity is not to load sin on us but to unload it.

Unexpiated guilt can be most disturbing. But confession is the solution. Having a lax conscience is a handicap, for it tends to cheat us out of a way in which we can be whole again. Sociologists have pointed out that suicide is less prevalent in countries where confession is readily available. Sin has the effect of causing us to withdraw from reality. The moral order demands realism. We should honor the Golden Rule and the Ten Commandments. Martin Buber held that sin is a violation of the "I-Thou" relationship. In other words, we sin when we are unjust to our neighbor. Realism demands brotherly love. Deviations from the rule of love move in the direction of unreality.

Guilt should be difficult to bear because it compromises one's friendship with God. "Be thou perfect as your heavenly Father is perfect" (Matthew 5:48) is, admittedly, a difficult standard to uphold. But it points in the right direction. It would be cruel only if forgiveness and mercy were not available. Christ wants us to be at our best. Guilt is a step backwards, but confession is a step forward.

A student once told me that the world would be in a better place if there were no guilt. He assumed that guilt was something like a virus that caused harm and is of no value. He was half right. On the one hand, if people did not recognize the evil of their evil actions, the world would be filled with unrepentant psychopaths. On the other hand, heaven is a place where there is neither sin nor guilt. But in this present world people will never be free of sin. There will always be a need for forgiveness. We can dream of the next world, but we must live in this one where sin abounds and Christianity is vitally needed.

Honesty, humility, and gratitude are a beautiful sequence of virtues. They are played out when we have the honesty to admit our sins, the humility to confess them, and the gratitude for receiving forgiveness. All this represents the positive side of guilt. On the negative side, people try to drown their guilt with alcohol or distract themselves from it through inordinate pleasures. These actions only multiply guilt since they give a person more reasons to be guilty.

Guilt is our message from God inviting us, like the Prodigal Son, to come home.

Nature vs. Nurture

Our 14th grandchild came into the world recently. Certainly, a joyous event. She is born of two human parents, a mother and a father. There is absolutely no doubt that she is a human being. But why should there be any doubt?

Liberal society has problems with limits. Being liberal, it naturally wants more of anything. Should marriage be restricted to two spouses? Are there more than two sexes? Should a woman marry a woman? Maybe there is more than one God. Transhumanists are hoping that technology will assist in boosting humans into a higher species. A student once posed the question to Mortimer Adler: "Is there more than one reality?" We might anticipate the notion that *Homo sapiens* will be divided into more than one species.

Strange as it may seem, there are well-known proponents of the idea that since there is no such thing as human nature, maybe there is a plurality of species included in what traditionally were called human beings. Jean-Paul Sartre stated emphatically that there is no such thing a human nature. And Merleau-Ponty asserted that "it is in the nature of man not to have a nature." Such thinkers find nature constraining. They believe that having a nature limits freedom. They maintain that human beings create their nature. This is an exciting prospect for those who make freedom absolute.

The unity of the human species is the basis for a human community. If there were a plurality of species included under *Homo sapiens*, a hierarchy would be inevitable. One species would be deemed superior to another. Human history is blighted by the prevalence of a master-slave mentality. If all men are equal, they are equal in their humanity and therefore neither higher nor lower than any other members of the species. The equality of all human beings under a single nature presupposes a common mind. There is but one mind, a human mind that is the same for all human beings.

The liberal love affair with diversity is wont to include that which does not belong. The so-called "open marriage" is really closed to a marriage between one man and one woman. A third party intruding on a loving marriage invites disaster. "Keeping to one woman," G. K. Chesterton noted, "is a small price for so much as seeing one woman. To complain that I could only be married once was like complaining that I had only been born once . . . Polygamy is a lack of the realization of sex."

If there is no common nature for all human beings, there is no common morality that creates the possibility of a human community. Warfare would be more frequent than ever before. Racism and various forms of prejudice are founded on at least the temptation that one group belongs to a higher species than another. Such an attitude would re-enact the ferocity between the fox and the hen.

The temptation to believe that human beings belong to different species lies in the fact that on both an individual and a cultural basis, human beings appear to be remarkably different. In the animal kingdom, lions, lizards, and lemmings show little variation within their respective groups. Each group is well defined by its species. In the case of man, custom, cuisine, clothing, and culture are patently different. Human beings speak over 1,000 different languages. Can each cultural group belong to the same *Homo sapiens* species?

This question is fully explained by introducing the word "nurture." Many try to understand the observable differences between human beings solely on the basis of nurture. But there must pre-exist something for nurture to act upon. And that which is acted upon is nature. If there is no nature, then there is no nurture. Mortimer Adler states simply and forcefully that "to confuse nature with nurture is a philosophical mistake of the first order." All human beings share the same nature. Yet they are subject to many different forms of nurturing. There are a hundred ways to cook spaghetti, but first you must have the spaghetti. And yet, if the spaghetti is not cooked, it is tasteless.

Shakespeare brilliantly illustrates the relationship between nature and nurture in his play *The Tempest.* Caliban is a monstrously-deformed inhabitant of a remote island. Prospero, the rightful Duke of Milan, finds himself on that island as a castaway. He describes Caliban as a "devil, a born devil, on whose nature nurture can never stick" (IV, i. 188-193). Caliban has the tragic misfortune of not being able to cultivate the good potentialities that are latent in his nature. He is incapable of receiving nurture. Shakespeare is affirming that Caliban has a nature, but at the same time he is indicating how the inability to receive of any kind of nurture turns him into a monster. We all know how critical it is for a newborn to be lovingly nurtured.

"Monsters will exist," writes American author and entrepreneur, Jacqueline Novogratz. "There's one inside each of us. But an angel lives there, too. There is no more important agenda than figuring out how to slay one and nurture the other."

In the nature/nurture debate, people ask which is more important. Neither is more important than the other since they are both necessary for the formation of a mature person. Our fourteenth grandchild will not become another Caliban. She has the good fortune of being born to happy, resourceful, and loving parents. If anything, she may be spoiled.

www.ingramcontent.com/pod-product-compliance
Lightning Source LLC
LaVergne TN
LVHW040220110826
845146LV00005B/1361

* 9 7 9 8 8 8 8 7 0 5 2 3 0 *